Emerging Word:
a Creation Spirituality Lectionary

*Scripture Readings and Commentary for the
Church Year*

Other books by Donald Schmidt

God's Paintbrush Celebration Kit
(with Rabbi Sandy Eisenberg Sasso)

Bible Wonderings: Familiar Tales Retold

In the Beginning: Creation Spirituality for the Days of Advent

Breaking Open: Creation Spirituality for the Weeks of Easter

Emerging Word:
a Creation Spirituality
Lectionary

*

Scripture Readings and Commentary
for the Church Year

Donald Schmidt

Emerging Word:
A Creation Spirituality Lectionary
Scripture Readings and Commentary
for the Church Year

Copyright © 2006, 2009 by Donald Schmidt

This book may be ordered from online booksellers, or directly from the author at www.emergingword.com

ISBN-13: 978-0-578-03628-1

Published by Corona
10235 SE 6th St.
Bellevue, WA 98004

Printed in the United States of America.

Dedication

To Bonnie and Pierre and others at United Theological College who first introduced me to Creation Spirituality, and challenged me to keep embracing new paradigms.

To my former colleagues at The Whole People of God *and* Seasons of the Spirit *who traveled with me through many, many cycles of the lectionary and liturgical year.*

To everyone at the University of Creation Spirituality (now Wisdom University), especially Matthew Fox, for having the vision to provide the amazing education that you offer, and that the world so much needs.

To Don whose endless conversations on theology and spirituality make life fascinating, whose encouragement kept me going when I wanted to give up, and whose love makes it all worthwhile.

Table of contents

"The Four Paths of Creation Spirituality help us live who we are."

Matthew Fox

Preface to the 2nd Edition

Since the publication of the first edition of this lectionary three years ago I have been surprised (okay, almost overwhelmed) by its popularity. It's not a bestseller by any means, but nonetheless it has been purchased and used by some 1,000 individuals and groups from Scotland to Australia, and many points in between.

It seems time for a second edition – firstly to fix the many typos in the first edition, but also to add a few pieces, such as a second set of lections for Christmas, "floaters" for the Season after Epiphany/Transformativa, and All Saints' Day. This is largely due to the feedback I have gotten from users, as well as from my own use of the lectionary.

However, even with all the changes, my underlying question has not changed: what if?

I've used that question to approach lots of things in life. Sometimes, I'll grant you, with less than desirable results but, most of the time, it leads to some wonderful imaginings. This book is the result of a "what if."

What if someone took the four paths of Creation Spirituality and overlaid them onto the traditional seasons of the Christian year? What sort of readings might emerge, and on what kind of spiritual journey might they take us?

There can be great value in taking tools and structures that exist – such as the liturgical year – and breathing new life, new form, and new possibility into them. Accordingly, for precisely this reason I wanted to explore taking the structure and form of the church year and the lectionary, and Creation Spirituality, and seeing what can happen when we merge the two together.

Of course myriad possibilities exist because there are not only many lectionaries but also many ways to structure them, and a variety of ways of looking at the liturgical year. Yet in all of the forms that have so far been employed, I would submit that overall they have been the product – or at best the servant – of a paradigm that does not speak as clearly to everyone in the church as it once did. To quote Matthew Fox, who is often described as the prophet of Creation Spirituality, "fall/redemption ideologies have so prevailed in theological scholarship that the very questions that are asked and not asked, the very translations of scriptures and of the mystics, the very meaning of holiness and the list of saints, have been dictated by this one stream of Christian tradition."[1] One could well add "the very lectionaries that have been structured" and even "the festivals of the liturgical year" have been dictated by this same stream as well.

My love affair with lectionaries (okay, how many people want to admit *that* kind of fetish?) goes back several years to when I began working as an editor with a lectionary–based worship and Christian education project. The resources were based on the readings of the Common Lectionary and later the Revised Common Lectionary, and our editorial team quickly became aware of the distinct advantages and disadvantages of using the lectionary as a device for telling the story of our faith – both as a tool for structuring worship, and also as a tool for structuring Christian education.

I continue to be a firm believer in the power of coordinating a church's ministry around common scriptures in order to provide an integrity to the work that is being done, to proclaim the gospel in word and sacrament and action. I also believe that the ecumenical aspect of using a common lectionary for such work is of great importance. I still think that the Revised Common Lectionary is a wonderful tool, its advantages far outweighing its disadvantages.

However, having said all that, I also came to recognize early on some of the disadvantages of the Revised Common Lectionary and others. The story being told by that lectionary grew out of what has been described variously as "fall/redemption theology" or the "early church paradigm" (more about these terms in chapter 1).

Alongside my fascination with lectionaries and the liturgical year has been my exploration of Creation Spirituality, which I first encountered in 1985 when I read Matthew Fox's *Original Blessing*. That book spoke to me like few others. Here on so many pages voice was being given to what I had thought, believed, pondered, experienced, dared to imagine, argued, dreamed.

---

[1] Matthew Fox, *Original Blessing: a Primer in Creation Spirituality*, (Santa Fe, New Mexico: Bear and Company, 1983), p. 27.

I converted.

No, let me rephrase that: I realized that I was not alone.

When I had the opportunity, in 2000, to begin a Doctor of Ministry degree at the University of Creation Spirituality (now Wisdom University) I leapt at the chance, and this lectionary is an adaptation of my dissertation.

I have used it at times to guide worship and study in my congregation. I have explored ways in which it challenges me to reconsider liturgical seasons and cycles of living and worshipping. I am aware that I have pushed some boundaries at times, but that's what this kind of work is about.[2]

So, what if we approached the church year in new ways? What if we took a different spiritual journey once in a while? What if we let scripture guide us in new ways once in a while?

What if?

Let's see...

---

[2] This is also the basis for my book *In the Beginning: Creation Spirituality for the Days of Advent* and my forthcoming *Breaking Open: Creation Spirituality for the Weeks of Easter.*

Chapter 1 – A brief introduction to Creation Spirituality

Much of the theology that is espoused in American–dominated society today uses a condensed Bible.[3] It tends to begin with the story of the Fall in Genesis 3, and end with the crucifixion. It is a theology that takes as its starting point an assumption that human beings are "miserable sinners" and concludes with Jesus "dying for our sins." While one can argue that those are parts of the spiritual journey, they are – according to scripture – neither the beginning nor the ending.

Matthew Fox has called this dominant theology "fall/redemption" theology and Marcus Borg refers to it as the "earlier" or "belief-centered" paradigm. In a less-scholarly book such as this where I don't have to be so polite, I would prefer to call it nonsense.

The Bible begins, not in Genesis 3, but in Genesis 1, where God creates the world and declares it to be good, the ultimate story of original blessing, not original sin. Beyond that the Christian story does not in fact end, but continues beyond crucifixion to resurrection, and into the transformation that takes place because of that.

Increasingly, people have come to question and challenge – or at least wonder about – this dominant theology. In its place are a

---

[3] I use the term "American-dominated" where one might use "Western" or "Euro-centric" or other terms that I believe are not quite accurate enough. Firstly, "Western" is far too relative a term that depends on where one is situated on the planet, or it implies an ethnocentrism that the "real" West is Europe and North America, regardless of where one is situated. This defies the logic of the planet. "Euro-centric" is historically no longer accurate; the reality is that the dominant culture in our world today, for better or worse, is that of the United States. Its philosophy, values, and theology are present virtually everywhere, being either adored, despised, tolerated, or on occasion debated. There are, of course, many other cultures of huge influence, sometimes greater influence, but the dominant one in many spheres at the current time seems to be American, at least loosely-defined.

number of "emerging paradigms" (to borrow again a phrase from Borg), one of which is Creation Spirituality.

Creation Spirituality is not so much a thing or an entity, as it is a canvass upon which one paints, a rhythm to which one is invited to dance, a theme song to accompany and harmonize with one's spiritual journey.

In many circles, when one mentions Creation Spirituality (if there is any point of recognition at all) the listener tends to nod and say, "oh, Matthew Fox."[4] There is no question that Fox has, more than any other, given voice to Creation Spirituality, inviting many into the dance and dialogue that it engenders. Matthew Fox also offers the world the many fruits of exploring not only Christianity but other faiths through the lens of a spirituality that takes creation seriously.

In *Original Blessing*, Fox's quintessential text subtitled "a Primer in Creation Spirituality presented in Four Paths," he speaks of Creation Spirituality as a tradition with strong historical and biblical roots. He then goes on to present it as a life–giving challenge to the fall/redemption paradigm that has dominated "western" society and thought for centuries.

Rather than beginning with original sin – a relatively late theological invention that, despite its popularity in some church circles, is *not* scriptural – Creation Spirituality begins with original blessing, which *is* scriptural. We stretch the Bible back to its beginning, to Genesis 1 and 2, stories of a God who created a world and declared it good; indeed, upon creating human beings, God declared the whole thing to be "very good" – Genesis 1:31. This is the same God who, while angry at the disobedience of the humans in the garden, does not kill them as threatened (Genesis 2:17) but is

---

[4] On a couple of occasions I have even found that people make a linguistic leap and readily equate Creation Spirituality with "creationism" or "creation science." It is important to distinguish between Creation Spirituality – which celebrates creation as original blessing – and the various conservative movements that espouse an attempt to twist the Bible into some sort of academic textbook. Such movements deny the realities of the cosmos, limit the arts, the imagination, and the sciences, and claim that the universe is a single, handmade object that came into being over six 24-hour days. This would belong to the "earlier paradigm."

so concerned for their well–being as to make clothes for them (Genesis 3:21) before sending them out into the world.

No person would show this kind of forgiveness, care, and compassion and then turn around centuries later and demand the death of their beloved child as payment for ancient disobedience; it's unthinkable that God would. Time and again the Bible reminds us that God gets angry with us – and rightly so – when we do in fact disobey God, move away from the divine will (what one might readily call "sin") but this is not our natural state. To base a key doctrine such as original sin on such a flimsy footing suggests that its proponents were, at best, desperate.

Similarly, Creation Spirituality tends toward a Christology of John 1, seeing Jesus as God's Word made flesh, a light shining in the darkness, revealing God's truth and light and love to *all* the world, without restriction and without end. Matthew Fox speaks of the "Cosmic Christ" as a way of understanding the divine essence, or Word (*logos* in Greek) "who lives and breathes in Jesus and *all* of God's children."[5]

The death of Jesus, then, is not payment for our wickedness but rather a radical way of showing God's ultimate triumph over the sinful powers of the empires of the world, and liberates us from fear. Fall/redemption theology – the earlier paradigm – has for centuries used fear of death (read: going to hell) to support imperialism. Early on, those who wanted to wield power over others discovered there was great benefit in promoting a theology that went something like this:

> We might have been good once, long ago, but we all became bad after one of us really messed up – Paul said it was Adam, but if we blame Eve, then we can blame women for everything as well. So anyway, we all became horrible, miserable and worthless, and have no hope in ever being anything else, because we're born that way. Except we have the right to dominate everything else in all creation because even though we're worthless, we're somehow better than everything else, because creation is all bad. But if you pray

5 Matthew Fox, *The Coming of the Cosmic Christ*, (San Francisco: Harper, 1988), p. 7

hard enough and believe hard enough (and we'll tell you how), Jesus will redeem you and you can be made right again. Amen.

Okay, I'm exaggerating. But sadly, not that much. Yet, while this sort of theology has often dominated in imperial circles – and that is hardly surprising, because it is a brilliant theology to support a power base – this is not the only theological understanding to present itself throughout Christian tradition. Beyond that, Creation Spirituality has enjoyed not only a long history, but a strong and profound scriptural basis as well. It finds its expression in four paths: *via positiva, via negativa, via creativa,* and *via transformativa.*

Exploring the four paths

Like points of a compass, the paths Creation Spirituality are not entities so much as touchstones in a circle, in a spiraling journey. They provide direction in a circular rather than linear way. Like the Hebrew *torah*, they are a guide or living way within which we can live and move and have our being, in conversation and co-creation with God.

One could use images other than paths. Some have spoken of four movements, rather like a symphony. Still others speak of four rooms, or fields. An image I have sometimes found helpful is to think of the four paths as overlapping circles, recognizing that we can on occasion be in different places at the same time. The names are not the issue – it's how we imagine ourselves taking the spiritual journey that matters.

The *Via Positiva:* Befriending Creation

The *via positiva* is a celebration of the fact that God created us, and declared us to be good – original blessing. It is awareness of creation, one's place in it, one's connectedness with it, and a celebration of the presence of God the Creator in the creation.

We need to be aware of the true wonder of all creation, and remember that we are very much a part of it. When we recognize that God made it, and loves it – rather than some sense that God made it, then abandoned it, or somehow despises it, and that we are above it or detached from it – the harmony that God intended can occur. We are far more inclined to respect, accept, and honor the creation, when we remember that the greatest and the smallest things is each one a necessary and beloved part of the whole. In the *via positiva*, as we celebrate creation, the universe and all within it – including our own bodies – are a blessing to be shared and enjoyed, not a curse to be borne and overcome.

The scriptures repeatedly remind us of God's intimate involvement in the history of the people God created and cares for despite everything. God repeatedly calls us to care for creation – which includes one another. (For some reason we keep forgetting that we are a part of creation; we tend to think of creation as an external "it," beyond ourselves.) It is worth noting that one of the most familiar passages of scripture – Psalm 23 – celebrates God's care for us in the midst of creation. John 3:16–17 reminds us that God loves the world to the extent of sending Jesus to save the world, not judge it. The Creator's love and concern for the creation is quite clear.

Thus we begin to see that, in the words of Julian of Norwich, "we have been loved from before the beginning."[6] We echo the words of Psalm 8 – "who are we, God, that you care for us?" – and we move into a state of humility. That is, we move willingly into true humility. Interesting, isn't it, that such a powerful word would be so misconstrued over the years. While the root of the word is *humus* (Latin for earth) to be humble is not to "feel like dirt" or to lie down on the ground to be trampled on. Rather, it is to be grounded, to be earthed, to find ourselves standing firmly on a foundation of God's handiwork, and see ourselves as neither above it or below it, but intrinsically part of it.

An awareness that God loves us opens up doorways to living that cannot be opened in any other way. The definition or attributes of the deity in question are secondary to the simple awareness of the divine as a part of us, and as our lover. No small wonder that in so many religious systems, the concept of earth as divine mother is so important.

---

[6] Cited in Matthew Fox, *Creation Spirituality: Liberating Gifts for the Peoples of the Earth,* (San Francisco: Harper, 1992), p. 28.

In Hebrew, the term *el shaddai* – most usually translated as "God of armies" or "of hosts" – comes from a Hebrew root connected with breasts, and alludes to the earth as divine breast from which we are given life and nurtured. How delightful, to think that a term often associated with macho might in English comes from a root that speaks of the epitome of strength being the ability to feed one's children. "Can a mother forget her nursing child?" God asks. "Yet even if she forgets, I will not forget you" (Isaiah 49:15). God loves us; we must love one another – and ourselves.

The love of self as original blessing is a concept not readily embraced in our society. The biblical admonition to "love your neighbor as you love yourself" often gets misinterpreted to imply that one should not love oneself. A popular slogan in conservative Christianity is "God first, others second, me last." Such an expression is often used, amongst other things, to convince women to stay in abusive relationships.

Jesus spoke of balance – loving God, neighbor and self as a kind of mobile, with equal weight given to all in order to achieve balance. Creation Spirituality affirms this. Conversely, living solely for the satiation of one's ego or belly is also frequently misunderstood as love of self.

This was clarified for me when I was listening, for the umpteenth time, to the airline safety announcement on a recent flight. "If you are traveling with a small child or someone needing assistance, secure your own oxygen mask before assisting others." To care for myself in such a basic way is not to be selfish, but to be realistic – if I do not love myself enough to take care of my own survival, I am not able to help another. It is that simple. In order to put that oxygen mask on myself before attempting to help a seatmate, I have to love myself enough, recognize in myself enough presence of the divine spark, to believe myself worthy of drawing breath. Without that I am pretty useless.

Likewise, I care for myself because I also want to help another – I see them as being as worthy of all of life's gifts and blessings as I myself. No more, no less. The Pali Canon of Buddhism speaks of how envy is that which does not celebrate the rising of another's qualities, but wants it only for oneself. The *via positiva* frees us from this envy, inviting us to celebrate and share original blessing.

The *Via Negativa:* Letting Go

This awareness of original blessing allows us to move beyond, to enter the looking-glass, to experience the *via negativa*. Not "negative" in the sense of denial of positive, but rather the opposite, the filling in of the blanks.

I like to think of the negative used in the old-fashioned process (now dying out) of making photographs. The negative is simply the opposite of the picture and a necessary part of the process. It is a way of letting the light shine through, a reverse mirror image and opposite way of seeing things.

Several years ago I had the great joy of attending the birth of my granddaughter. All the waiting, all the wondering, and the ever-widening belly of my daughter reminded us of pending newness. Then after struggling and pain my granddaughter appeared. Her eyes wide as noonday suns tried to absorb all the weird reality of her new state of being. She had spent nine months in total darkness in which she prepared to be born. Now she was in a new, exciting, and frightening world of light.

We all need that darkness. We all need times of silence, of aloneness, of nothingness – not so easily done in our world of noise and busyness.

In the *via negativa* we learn to let go and embrace the dark. It's not always easy. If, for example, you say "I must stop thinking about chocolate" you'll only think about chocolate all the more.

Yet let go we must: we must sleep; we must dream; we must allow ourselves simply to be; we must dare to embrace that which would threaten and frighten us. Such conscious embracing of pain, and of consciously letting it go, is a vital part of the sacred journey. Systems that deny this step in the journey are gravely flawed. There is no sunrise without sunset, no Easter without Good Friday, no new life without the pains of childbirth.

I once visited a wildlife park and learned about what goes on inside a cocoon. I had always assumed that the caterpillar, once inside the cocoon, simply changed. It donned wings and antennae and slimmed down a bit, but otherwise remaining intact – rather like Clark Kent dashing into the phone booth to become Superman. I was quite surprised to learn that the caterpillar becomes a swirling, icky liquid mass, and from this "formless void" (to quote Genesis 1) comes the butterfly. This is the *via negativa,* the process that leads us to birth.

The most powerful – and lasting – image for me of the *via negativa* is one that Matthew Fox presents in *Original Blessing,* borrowing from Japanese poet Kenji Miyazawa. It is an image of embracing pain like a bundle of kindling for a fire. We hold it, we carry it for a time, we thrust it on the fire, letting it go, and in turn we receive benefit from the warmth and light it can provide us.[7]

This is the manner in which we can and indeed *must* deal with our pain. First comes the embrace, the allowing of pain to be pain; next comes the journey with the pain; then the letting go, but in a deliberate manner, into a fire, into a cauldron where the pain's energy will serve us. Finally comes the benefit we do indeed derive from having burned this fuel. Pain is meant to give us energy.

The *Via Creativa:* Embracing our Divinity

"Where our clinging to things ends is where God begins to be," says Meister Eckhart.[8] This is breakthrough. This is what Creation Spirituality calls the beginning of the *via creativa.* It is the point at which one allows God to enter. As Leonard Cohen says, "There is a crack in everything / that's how the light gets in."[9]

If *via positiva* is conception, and *via negativa* is gestation, then *via creativa* is the birthing process. Both Fox and Eckhart remind us of the need for all of us to give birth – not literally, of course, but figuratively. We are called upon to birth God's presence continually in our world. This is what Eckhart presumably had in mind when he first coined the term "breakthrough." When we allow ourselves to be a part of creation, and when we are able to embrace the dark and let go of pain, we find ourselves open. When we are open, birth can take place.

---

[7] Fox, *Original Blessing*, pp. 142–143.

[8] Cited in Matthew Fox, *A Spirituality Named Compassion*, (Rochester, VT: Inner Traditions, 1999), p. 91.

[9] "Anthem" in Leonard Cohen, *Stranger Music*, (Toronto: McClelland and Stewart, 1993), p. 373.

We are creative beings, and yet so often we have denied our creativity. Or we deny it in others. Or we believe those who tell us we are not, or cannot, be creative. Yet we are made in the image of God and God is nothing if not a creator. To be creative in a god-like way is to celebrate what has been created, including ourselves, and to open ourselves to the life possibilities within each of us. When we balance ourselves in the night and the day, the dark and the light, we allow new birth to break open within us and through us.

In turn, through our creating we are transformed. Through celebrating creation, daring the dark, and giving birth to new realities, we find ourselves in compassion. In being creative, as God is creative, we learn also what it is to be compassionate, as God is compassionate.

We no longer see ourselves in relationship with other people as subject/object, but as equals. We do not see ourselves as saviors of others – us helping them – but as those who will join one another in our living.

We suffer with. We journey with. We live with. We *be* with.

Breakthrough comes when we move from pity to compassion. The Dalai Lama reminds us that "any love or compassion which entails looking down on the other is not genuine compassion. To be genuine, compassion must be based on respect for the other, and on the realization that others have the right to be happy and overcome suffering just as much as you. On this basis, since you can see that others are suffering, you develop a genuine sense of concern for them."[10]

When we experience breakthrough, when we allow God in, amazing things happen. We see, feel, and live in new ways, and we begin to act differently. All the world begins to be transformed, if ever so slightly.

---

[10] His Holiness the XIV Dalai Lama, *The Four Noble Truths*, translated by Geshe Thupten Jinpa (London: Thorsons, 1997), pp. 134–135.

The *Via Transformativa:* Compassion, Celebration, and Justice

In the *via transformativa* we find ourselves reconciled to new realities, to ourselves, to the world around us. We receive and share, shape and are shaped by new insight. We seek justice and love kindness and walk humbly with our God. We recognize anew our interdependence with other aspects of creation, and so we are transformed. Yet we have not "arrived," for this journey is not one about completion, but of re-journeying.

The dictionary is both helpful and ambiguous here. *Com* is the Latin word for *with*. But *passion* stems from *passus*, which has roots in both suffering and walking. Which came first? The most commonly-accepted source for the English word *compassion* is the sense of sharing suffering. However, the sense of "walking together" in terms of sharing a journey, or walking a proverbial mile in another's shoes, is a wonderful way of understanding the *via transformativa* as well.

The *via transformativa* is a communal thing. To quote the old UNICEF slogan, "until all of us have made it, none of us have." Or, as Matthew Fox puts it, "what the *via transformativa* makes abundantly clear is the biblical teaching that in fact there is no such thing as privatized or individualized salvation."[11] This latter is a fairly modern notion, born largely out of the industrial revolution and a more recent sense of rugged individualism and frontierism. But the sense of "every man for himself" (and I think we can let the inherent sexism of that statement stand, because I want to throw the statement out anyway) does not really jive with biblical teaching, which constantly calls us to a life of compassion. "Am I my brother's keeper?" Cain asked. To which the answer is a resounding "yes." Who is our brother? Whoever does the will of God, says Jesus, "is my brother and sister and mother" (Matthew 12:50).

This transformation of our individual selves and our world happens in the context of compassion, of seeing ourselves as an integral part of God's creation – neither detached from it nor superior to it, but part of it. Only if we *want* to be in relationship

---

[11] Fox, *Original Blessing*, p. 297.

with our brothers and sisters – animal (including human), vegetable, and mineral – can we hope to be agents of good in our world. Any effort to tame, control, or subdue creation, instead of living in harmony with it, is self-defeating. As the advertisements for energy conservation used to say, "if you're not part of the solution, you're part of the problem."

We reach beyond ourselves. The transformation that we have experienced stretches beyond us, like ripples in a pond. It is unavoidable. As we have received and experienced God's grace, so we cannot help but share it. Forgiveness, compassion, and a zeal for justice flow forth from within us; it is what Buddhists would call *bodhicitta*.

A word needs to be said here about an oxymoron that gets tossed about, namely "compassionate conservatism." This tragi-comic conflict in terms conjures up a sense of taking pity on those "less fortunate," and such a thing is not compassion. This is where following the four paths is helpful, and indeed vital. Compassionate conservatism invites us to bypass them, and to remain in a sense of duality, a subject/object relationship in which I can stay on my mountaintop and pity those down below. In that context, I do not grow spiritually, and nothing/no one is transformed. Yet this notion seems to have reached a deafening crescendo in recent times.

The combination of greed and fear that appear to fuel each other and propel society ever further away from community and towards isolation must feed on contradiction, and so compassionate conservatism seems to serve well. A payment of noisy lip service to a deity while flagrantly disregarding the teachings of same is the perpetual stuff of empires. As Eckhart pointed out in Sermon 14, "some people want to love God in the same way as they love a cow. You love it for the milk and the cheese and for your own profit. So do all people who love God for the sake of outward riches or inward consolation. But they do not love God correctly, for they merely love their own advantage."[12]

---

[12] Matthew Fox, *Passion for Creation: the Earth-Honoring Spirituality of Meister Eckhart*, (Rochester, VT: 2000), p. 207.

The Protestant work ethic mentality (which somehow had room in it for Roman Catholics and Jews and, by extension, even those in the "none of the above" category as long as they behaved like "real Americans") dominated the second half of the twentieth century. It counted primarily on us having an enemy (thank God for the USSR), objects of pity (those starving brown–skinned children haunting prime-time infomercials) and a sense of purpose or a sense of drive.

Yet compassion – love of God and love of neighbor, in the words of the Hebrew and Christian scriptures – is not about what we can get. Nor is it about what we can give. It is about how we *be*. I am reminded of a poem that I learned in Sunday school as a child. I don't remember the first few lines, but the gist was to list several biblical characters and point out their wrongdoings. It is the ending, however, that I do recall:

"Your wasness doesn't matter, if your isness really am."

That's the point of the *via transformativa*. That's the point of the four paths.

Why do we need Creation Spirituality?

Creation Spirituality offers – and calls us to – a life that is transformed and transforming. It allows for real transformation, for real change. And there is hardly any question that our world is in desperate need of a radical transformation of the heart. As individuals, communities, nations, and global community we hunger for compassion.

This hunger for compassion, and for a way to explore both compassion and the transformation that it engenders, is at the heart of other hugely popular writings and movements (such as *The Celestine Prophecies*) calling for the rejection of old paradigms and the embracing of new ones. Creation Spirituality is not unique, nor does it provide all the answers. What does give it merit, however, is that in giving it voice, Matthew Fox has grounded it in historical, biblical, and theological roots. Rather than simply saying "I think this is a good idea and you need to get on board" he has painstakingly shown that Creation Spirituality is not new – not in the least. It is ancient, and yet it speaks in the freshest, boldest ways to a world that is stale and hungry.

In first giving form and voice to Creation Spirituality in the early 1980's, Matthew Fox provided several reasons for the need to reclaim this ancient paradigm for our current world. He included such things as scientific awakening, ecological and unemployment crises, justice and liberation movements, and a general need for religious and educational transformation.

Now, almost a quarter century later, the world has changed. The church has changed, and yet the hunger remains.

Marcus Borg speaks of an "emerging paradigm" or new way of understanding, defining, and being Christian that is needed to replace the earlier paradigm that has stopped speaking to many people. At best it has outlived its purpose; at its worst, caused a great deal of harm.[13]

The emerging paradigm to which Borg refers is one that understands the Bible as a human response to God, seeing it as a metaphor and a sacrament, a means of understanding our relationship with God. More importantly, the emphasis of the Christian life is that we are to be transformed, in this life, through our relationship with God. What is that, if it is not the *via transformativa*?

Creation Spirituality, as a paradigm in itself, seeks to invite us into transforming relationship with God, and with one another. It can be life giving and rejuvenating. "It has the power to birth people anew, and with that birthing to rebirth structures and ways of living."[14]

_____

[13] Borg is not the first, nor the only, one to use the term "emerging" (witness the title of this book, for example). However, I find his definition and use of "emerging paradigm" to be the one that is most helpful to what is needed in the church at this point in time, and complements the work done by Fox immeasurably. See especially Borg's *The Heart of Christianity: Rediscovering a Life of Faith* (San Francisco: Harper, 2003). Interestingly, a few years later Borg changed the term "emerging paradigm" to "belief-centered paradigm" (see Mike Schwarzentruber's *The Emerging Christian Way: Thoughts, Stories, and Wisdom for a Faith of Transformation,* (Kelowna, BC: Copper House, 2006).

[14] Fox, *Original Blessing,* p. 25.

Chapter 2 – An Overview of the Christian Year

Like the lectionary, the Christian year tells a story by itself. It has its own inherent logic and pattern – and thus its own set of limitations, too. As parish minister and writer Shelley Cochran puts it, the church year "carries with it certain assumptions and operating principles that prefer certain themes and emphases in the Christian faith over others" being "unapologetically a yearly rehearsal of the life of Christ."[15]

Beyond that, it is essentially the life of Christ according to Luke, in that it begins with Advent, a concept that probably would not exist were it not for Luke's gospel and its extensive pre-birth stories, combined with a rather detailed birth narrative. The 12-day season of Christmas is traditionally framed by two stories of the birth of Jesus: Luke's account of the infant Jesus discovered by shepherds, and Matthew's story of a toddler Jesus worshipped by foreigners. This latter story then gives way to the Season after the Epiphany, known as Ordinary Time in some traditions.

The Lent/Easter cycle, being the most ancient liturgical season in the history of the church, has its origins in the ancient practice of Easter baptism and the preparation of persons to be baptized. However, the extension of Easter into fifty days leading up to Pentecost is due again to Luke's account of Pentecost in the second chapter of Acts. The remainder of the church year is, for all intents and purposes, "filler" as we impatiently wait for Advent to start the whole thing over again.

The great length of this rather bland second half of the year has given rise to various innovations, none of which has had much ecumenical shelf life. In 1937 the former Federal Council of Churches in the US advocated calling the season from Trinity Sunday until Advent Kingdomtide. Three years later, they modified this, suggesting that Kingdomtide begin on the last Sunday of August. The only denomination to pick this up and run with it was the Methodist Church, including the season in worship books

---

[15] Shelley Cochran, *The Pastor's Underground Guide to the Revised Common Lectionary: Year A,* (St. Louis: Chalice Press, 1995), pp. 24 and 34.

published in 1944 and 1965. A few other Protestant denominations also included Kingdomtide for a while, but none with any great enthusiasm and, when the United Methodist Church produced a *Book of Worship* in 1992, Kingdomtide (which had all been forgotten) was nowhere to be found.

In a similar vein, Scottish liturgical scholar Allan A. McArthur advocated a more Trinitarian approach to the entire church year, yielding up the festival half to Christ, the weeks after Pentecost to the Holy Spirit, and offering the second half of Ordinary Time (from the last Sunday of August again) to "God the Father." American Presbyterians tried this from 1956–1960, but then abandoned it.

Perhaps more intriguing still is the United Church of Canada's adaptation of McArthur's suggestion, which resulted in a Season of Creation, also beginning the last Sunday of August. This was included in their 1969 worship book and lectionary. Had this volume achieved wider use, the season might have grown in popularity. However, the idea of using a bound worship book was considered too alien for many in this denomination, and the lectionary, while innovative, quickly gave way to the Common Lectionary and this Season of Creation fell by the proverbial wayside.

More recently, Dr. Norman Habel of Adelaide, South Australia, one of the founders of the *Earth Bible* project, has advocated a shorter Season of Creation that is growing in international and ecumenical popularity. This Season of Creation begins September 1 and lasts for the four Sundays continuing a few weeks after the feast of St. Francis of Assisi (October 4). Much shorter than the one proposed some thirty years before in Canada, this season can provide an intriguing respite in an otherwise long (and for some, dreary) season of ordinary time. [16]

Prior to this, Sr. Margie Abbott (also from Adelaide) divided the church year into four seasons and paired these with the four primal elements and the four paths of Creation Spirituality. In addition, because this was done in the southern hemisphere it provided

---

[16] For more information on the lectionaries that were created for these seasons, see *Appendix 1.*

further challenge to the traditional perceptions and biases of a liturgical year that was developed, and is firmly entrenched, in the natural cycles of the northern hemisphere.

The seasons in Abbott's calendar match up like this:

> **Earth** – Way of Awe and Wonder *(Via Positiva)* – winter, south, strength, Ordinary Time
>
> **Air** – Way of Release *(Via Negativa)* – spring, east, truth, Ordinary Time
>
> **Water** – Way of Creative Imagination *(Via Creativa)* – summer, north, love, Advent/Christmas/Epiphany/Ordinary Time
>
> **Fire** – Way of Conversion and Action *(Via Transformativa)* – autumn, west, beauty, Lent/Easter/Pentecost[17]

Like the traditional church year, Abbott has begun in the winter; however, it is the southern winter, and thus she begins in Ordinary Time (Season after Pentecost).

There are obviously still more ways of living within the rhythms of the Christian year. It is not an entity meant to bind us, but rather a framework within which to live out our faith story each year.

In this lectionary, I will follow the "traditional" year of Advent through Ordinary Time, adapting it and blending it with Creation Spirituality in these ways:

- **Advent** – the four Sundays leading up to December 25 will be given over to an introduction to the four paths (Advent 1 = *Via Positiva;* Advent 2 = *Via Negativa,* Advent 3 = *Via Creativa;* and Advent 4 = *Via Transformativa*). This provides an opportunity to introduce the themes of Creation Spirituality at the beginning of the year and to ground us in them while at the same time moving Advent away from merely longing and waiting for redemption. The sense of

---

[17] Margie Abbott RSM, *Sparks of the Cosmos: Rituals for Seasonal Use* (Unley, South Australia: Mediacom Education, 2001).

anticipation can be instead for unbridled celebration of the incarnation.[18]

- **Christmas** and **Epiphany** – from the festival of the birth of Christ up to Lent, we celebrate the *via positiva*, the goodness of creation, our part in it, and the wonders of original blessing.

- **Lent** – this is a logical time for encountering the *via negativa*. This does not mean that, as in days past, we give ourselves over to guilt and shame but rather that, in the context of Creation Spirituality, we embrace the negative. We can do so having firmly grounded ourselves in the *via positiva* already.

- **Easter** – the marriage of *via positiva* and *via negativa* gives birth to the *via creativa* which comes to logical celebration in the great fifty days of Easter. From the festival of resurrection through the feast of Pentecost we celebrate breakthrough.

- **The Season of Transformation** – the work of the Holy Spirit in our midst is lived out through the *via transformativa*, and this is logically lived out liturgically through "ordinary time" when we seek to be transformed and transforming, in light of the previous three paths.

Throughout this whole cycle, festival days are kept to an absolute minimum. The biggest reason for this was not knowing where to end. The vast number of days observed by the ecumenical community, or by one tradition and not another, poses simply too many challenges to the flow of the year to render a one-year, experimental lectionary pretty useless. Observing various festivals within the context of Creation Spirituality does have its own merit, however. Maybe another time…

In this volume I have included a minimal number: Christmas, Epiphany, Ash Wednesday, Holy Week/Easter, Pentecost. I have expanded Trinity Sunday and renamed it "The Festival of the Names of God" which seemed both more scriptural and more in keeping with Creation Spirituality. Also, in this updated version of

---

[18] For a more expansive treatment of these concepts see my book *In the Beginning: Creation Spirituality for the Days of Advent*, (iUniverse, 2007).

the book I have – at the request of several users – included readings for All Saints' Day.

Chapter 3 – Choosing Scriptures

The Roman Catholic and Revised Common lectionaries tend toward Hebrew scripture, Psalm, Epistle, and Gospel (although even that pattern has its exceptions). However, while any structure is of course arbitrary, the specific Old Testament/New Testament balance inherent in this pattern invite its rejection along with its deep-rootedness in the fall/redemption theology that belongs to the earlier paradigm of the church's life. The employment of a different pattern would immediately invite a new way of looking at familiar texts.

I chose the traditional divisions of the Hebrew scriptures – Torah, Prophets, and Writings – and added Gospel as the fourth reading for each week. However, I have in turn chosen some variations on these themes. Clearly this pushes the proverbial envelope. I beg to use in my defense, however, the fact that one does have to wonder at least a little bit about some of the traditional divisions in the Bible itself. For example, why are the census figures of Numbers considered Torah? Why is Jonah, long considered a work of fiction by the ancient rabbis, included as a prophet?

Thus, in a given week in this lectionary, any number of the readings may come from either the Hebrew scriptures or a portion of the New Testament, following the pattern of Torah, Writing, Prophet, and Gospel. Simply the way in which we label a text invites us to read it anew, such as calling Mary of Nazareth a prophet (Advent 4 and Transformativa 15).

The length of readings varies substantially, and I do not know of a way around this, without doing some of the texts a severe injustice. On occasion, one can extract and discard verses without causing serious problems. In general I took for a guide the principles used by the Vatican II editors, who omitted things such as stage directions, names that were not important to the context, non-essential information, harsh verses, and things that would alter the context in the case of readings chosen for thematic purposes – all the while recognizing that this is, of course, highly subjective.

At the same time, however, it is difficult to break up certain passages. The story of Jonah really needs to be told in its entirety, and yet that makes for a very long reading. On the other hand, John's prologue is usually read as one piece and I have intentionally broken it into two smaller bites, as it were: John 1:1–5, and 6–18. Further, the gospel reading for Lent 1 (Mark 1:14–15) may seem ridiculously short but, well, that's the piece that works for that particular Sunday; why add to it?

Here are the ways I have – roughly – divided the scriptures for the purpose of this lectionary:

Torah – Primarily the first five books of the Hebrew scriptures. However, I have also included occasionally some teachings of Jesus as Torah. This is not to diminish Hebrew Torah, nor to supplant it with Jesus, but first and foremost to recognize the Jewishness of Jesus. Secondly, this recognizes Jesus' own proclamation of his teaching as potential supplement to the Torah. Lastly, this invites us to wonder what happens when we juxtapose the teachings of Rabbi Jesus with the teachings of the Torah, and ponder them in that light.

I have also, in the season of Lent, substituted the story of David from 1 Samuel for the Torah readings, to provide an opportunity to focus on that story in the context of the *via negative*. I have occasionally included a few other pieces from Hebrew scripture as well.

Prophets Primarily, these texts are taken from the Hebrew prophets. However, on occasion they are taken from New Testament readings, such as the epistles, and the teachings of prophets such as John the Baptizer and Mary of Nazareth. I have also included the stories of key prophetic acts from other books of scripture, such as the stories of Vashti and Esther, and what I would call the "awakenings" of Paul and Peter from the Book of Acts. The Revelation to John is also included in this category – not for the mistaken sense that prophets foretell the future but rather that prophets speak to the urgency of the times, and read the present reality. Most definitely the book of Revelation does that.

Writings In addition to the traditional Hebrew texts such as Psalms, Proverbs, and others, this is where I have often included portions of the epistles.

Gospels Just as all of scripture is writing, is prophetic, and describes God's way *(torah)*, so it could be argued that it all proclaims gospel or good news. However, for the purpose of this lectionary I have chosen only to include five gospels: Matthew, Mark, Luke, John, and the Acts of the Apostles. This last is included in this category as, according to its author, it forms a second volume of a larger work, a continuation of the good news of the first book we have come to call "Luke" and thus, I believe, ought to be included in the same category.

I chose not to include any apocryphal readings, with the exception being John 8:1–11, which most scholars consider to be an addition to the original text. I also resisted a strong desire to include a fifth reading from non-scriptural literature for each Sunday, as I believe that would shift the focus.

Like any lectionary, this presents a framework within which to set up a series of scripture readings for preaching, study, spiritual enhancement, for reflection, for growth, for contemplation. The intent being, in this case, that these readings will guide one along the paths of Creation Spirituality.

All of this is done with the corollary that no lectionary is "neutral" or objective. Each has an agenda. They set out to tell a story, or to serve a purpose. There is nothing inherently right or wrong about this, but it needs to be stated and owned. And, accordingly, we must approach any lectionary with caution and a hermeneutic of suspicion.

This is as good a place as any to remind you that this lectionary is little more than an experiment in proof-texting. In fact, it is quite shameless proof-texting. I have taken a huge number of my favorite scriptures, and arranged them rather neatly to serve my purposes.

Yet I don't think that that renders this exercise completely invalid. It is simply a caution. Any lectionary sets out to prove a point, as it were. This one does so at the hand of an individual, rather than a denominational or ecumenical council, and so that makes it a little more suspect.

Having said that, however, I would hope that the pattern of scriptures chosen in this lectionary can provide a fresh vehicle for encountering God through a yearly cycle, intentionally encountering and exploring the four paths in the process, while dancing among the liturgical seasons, and doing all of this with an eye and ear and heart to Creation Spirituality. Like any good lectionary or other liturgical tool it provides a method for challenging us in our worship and devotional lives. It lets scripture companion us as a church to explore new dimensions of God in our midst – through the incarnate Christ, the cosmic Christ, the living Christ.

Matthew Fox asks, "Can the churches themselves believe enough in the resurrection and in Pentecost to be resurrection and to become awakeners of the Spirit?"[19] It is my hope that this lectionary – even just as a spark for discussion – might help move us a little in that direction.

---

[19] Fox, *Cosmic Christ*, p. 8.

Chapter 4 – Advent: the Season of Anticipation

Each of the four Sundays of Advent will be used to introduce one of the themes of Creation Spirituality:

Advent 1 – *via positiva*

Advent 2 – *via negativa*

Advent 3 – *via creativa*

Advent 4 – *via transformativa*

In this way, the church year is immediately set within the context of the four paths, and the themes of Creation Spirituality are presented as an entrée to the liturgical year. This also neatly anticipates both the entire year, and the breakthrough presented by the incarnation that challenges our sensibilities and invites us into the unique relationship with God that is presented to us in Jesus Christ, however we wish to understand and undertake that relationship. At the same time, this takes the emphasis of Advent away from being a series of readings of the Hebrew prophets that may be seen to anticipate or even, in the worst-case scenario, predict the birth of Christ.

ADVENT 1 *(via positiva)*

Torah	Genesis 1:1–2:4a (4b–25)
Writing	Proverbs 8:22–31
Prophet	Isaiah 40:1–10
Gospel	John 1:1–5

We begin with creation. We begin "in the beginning," with a story of God's word piercing the primeval *tohu v'vohu* (the Hebrew expression traditionally translated *formless void*, although more literally akin to *gobbledygook)* and challenging it with life. The spirit of God *(ruach)* that hovers here and births/speaks/draws forth creation is not separate from the creation, but intrinsically a part of it. Theologian Norm Habel speaks of God's spirit waiting in the darkness and how "this story of creation embraces the presence of God as an integral part of the cosmos, perpetually moving within the cosmos."[20] God isn't out there, but in here.

While it is doubtful that anyone would read through the second creation story as well, it seems appropriate to offer it as an option, simply because it would be a shame not to include it. However, the first story is key for the *via positiva*. The apparent equality of men and women in the created order, combined with the power of God's Word and the repeated declaration of all things as good recommend it. More importantly, this is the quintessential text to begin a journey of Creation Spirituality. This is where the Judeo-Christian story begins, and it is clearly, undeniably – and scripturally – grounded firmly in original blessing.

Two other creation stories complement this first one. The first comes from Proverbs and includes the delightful imagery of Wisdom playing alongside the creator – as a key architect in some translations, and as a small child in others. Both translations are equally legitimate, and invite intriguing reflection.

---

[20] Norman Habel, "Geophany: The Earth Story in Genesis 1," in Habel and Wurst, *Earth Bible Two*, pp. 36–37. Habel further cites N. Wyatt "The Darkness in Genesis 1.2", *Vetus Testamentum* 43: 543–54.

This in turn is juxtaposed with the opening verses of John's prologue, a combination creation story/birth narrative of the cosmic Christ.

I have split the traditional passage of John 1:1–18, so that here we might focus solely on the arrival of the Word as the source of life. John affirms that the very word of God, which was the essence of God's creative energy in the beginning of everything in Genesis, has now been made flesh in Jesus – the cosmic Christ, now present on earth. This same Word is understood as the logical (derived from *logos*, meaning Word in Greek) expression of God's wisdom. The remainder of John's prologue will be used in the Season after the Epiphany.

The one "traditional" Advent text in the set, Isaiah 40, with its words of comfort and hope, rounds out the celebration of creation and blessing that begins us on this liturgical adventure.

The intent of this combination of readings is to capture the essence of the *via positiva,* and set a tone for the season and the year: creation is good, God's promise is for goodness, and there is hope in the word of God. The inherent goodness of creation, exemplified in God's word/Word and promise, has been present from the beginning, and will be forever. This is the essence of the message of the entire cycle of the church year.

ADVENT 2 *(via negativa)*

Torah	Matthew 24:3–14
Writing	Philippians 2:5–11
Prophet	Hosea11:1–11
Gospel	Matthew 3:1–12

Here one will notice the use both of a traditional Gospel text as Torah, and of a passage from the New Testament used for the Writing.

In Matthew 24:3–14 Jesus challenges the disciples to think outside the box in terms of the end of the world. When will it happen? One day, yes, but long, long down the road. Bad things will happen – horrible things, in fact – and the disciples will experience torture and mistreatment. But the gospel will continue to be proclaimed to all the world. Then, and only then, will things come to an end.

Certainly the most central text in the *via negativa* context of "pouring out" is the great hymn in praise of Christ from Philippians. This text connects the cross with the incarnation, and in this image of pouring out we prepare for indwelling, for we can only be filled with the new when we first empty ourselves. While this is probably not what Isaac Watts had in mind when penning "Joy to the World," the *via negativa* is a marvelous way for us to "let every heart prepare a room."

The other texts revolve more around the theme of being distanced from God and in turn the consequences of returning to God, whether this return be of human or divine initiation. The Hosea passage provides the back and forth sense of God's tension with us – "I love you, and you disobey me to the point where I want to destroy you, and yet I love you, and you disobey me, and yet…" How do we live in this tension?

The call to repentance issued by John the Baptizer is a summons to let go, to turn away from one set of values, and toward God. To repent is to take the opportunity to turn away from the old and turn towards the new. This opportunity to start again is a wondrous gift. In turning – and re-turning – to God we experience forgiveness, which is an essential part of the salvation journey.

"Forgiveness is another word for letting go," writes Matthew Fox in describing the *via negativa*. "We are saved by forgiveness, the power to forgive ourselves, to allow ourselves to be forgiven."[21]

---

[21] Fox, *Original Blessing*, p. 163.

ADVENT 3 *(via creativa)*

Torah	Genesis 9:8–17
Writing	Romans 8:14–22 (23–25)
Prophet	Isaiah 2:1–5
Gospel	Luke 4:16–21

The birthing imagery of Romans 8 (read at Trinity Sunday in other lectionaries) introduces us to the *via creativa*. The theme of breakthrough is especially enhanced by JB Philips' translation of v. 19, "the whole creation stands on tiptoe to see the children of God coming into their own."

My preference is to end the passage at verse 22; however, in some translations (notably the NRSV) this means stopping mid-sentence, which is not recommended, and so the remaining verses of the paragraph are included as an option. Likewise, starting at verse 14 can be problematic in at least one translation – the *New International Version* – as it begins mid-sentence. However, this is still at a logical break: "For those…"

Juxtaposed with this is God's promise to all living beings, epitomized in the symbol of the rainbow. It is so important, in this Advent season, to note the significance of this early covenant in Genesis, a passage that contains a form of the Hebrew word for "life" a total of six times. Similarly, it is noteworthy that there is not one covenant with humankind and another with the "rest of creation" but rather one covenant with all of creation. In fact, in Genesis 9:13 it is simply described as being between "God and the earth." This is a key aspect of original blessing – God has made a covenant with all creation, of which humankind is an intrinsic part. Too often there is a tendency to speak of "us" and "creation" as if we were somehow separate from it.

Both the Isaiah and Luke readings speak for themselves as imaginative or *via creativa* texts. While it may at first glance seem peculiar to read a passage from the life of Jesus during Advent, it really is no more out of the ordinary than to read of the adult life of John the Baptizer, or of the adult Jesus speaking of the end of time, which is traditionally done on Advent 1 and which I have included on Advent 2.

ADVENT 4 *(via transformativa)*

Torah	Matthew 1:1–17
Writing	1 John 4:7–21
Prophet	Luke 1:46–55
Gospel	Matthew 1:18–25

This week's readings challenge merely by their presentation: the genealogy from Matthew, seldom read at all let alone in worship, is a powerful text by virtue of the names themselves. The inclusion of women and foreigners tells us much of the nature of God and the Messiah who is about to be born. This background serves as the Torah reading, and the narrative continuation of the passage serves in turn as the Gospel reading.

Here we meet Joseph, adoptive father of Jesus, who intentionally chooses to break biblical law and social custom to save Mary's life. What a potent foretaste to the transforming ministry of the soon-to-be-born Messiah!

In between are presented 1 John's mini-sermon on the nature of love, and the great sermon of Mary of Nazareth, here given its proper place as a prophetic reading.

While the Magnificat is often read on this Sunday, reading it as the "prophetic" text may help to demythologize Mary a little, and allow her to be the prophet of Creation Spirituality that she truly is. Too many centuries of piety (and, I would submit, a very intentional effort to make her a model of nothing but sexual abstinence, mindless obedience, child-bearing, and child-rearing) have distanced Mary from her revolutionary words and actions, and all of Christianity has suffered for it. Accordingly, this text will be repeated in its entirety in this lectionary, appearing again on Transformativa 15.

Chapter 5 – *Via Positiva:* Christmas and Epiphany

The Gospel readings for the festival days Christmas and Epiphany are obviously dictated by the days themselves. However, the choice of other readings can help to set the observance of the festivals more fully within the pathway of the *via positiva*.

CHRISTMAS EVE

Torah	Deuteronomy 6:4–9
Writing	Psalm 148
Prophet	Isaiah 9:2–7
Gospel	Luke 2:1–7 (8–20)

The Prophet and Gospel texts are obvious in their choices. Similarly the Writing, while usually reserved for the Sunday after Christmas, fits the theme of *via positiva* well with its unbridled celebration of all creation praising God.

The choice of Deuteronomy is to connect the birth of Jesus with the heritage of our faith in the essentials of Judaism, recognizing the Jewishness of Jesus and of the roots of Christianity. Within the context of remembering the oneness of God, and the commandment to love God with all of our being, we celebrate the birth of the one we would understand as the Messiah for our time and place.

This is in no way to imply a supplanting of Christianity over Judaism, nor a declaration of an exclusive understanding of Christic salvation, but rather a clear grounding of Christian celebration within the inherent Judaism of our scriptures and our faith. Indeed repeatedly throughout the Christian year, in our worship and ritual and storytelling, we need to embrace a deep ecumenism. We must reclaim the Jewishness of our own spiritual tradition as well as the inherent link of all spiritual traditions. Our story is not ours alone. Even as we proclaim "Hear, O people, our God is one..." with the writer(s) of Deuteronomy, we recall that the manifestations, understandings, and images of that same God are myriad, and worthy of many forms of celebration.

On this day, we celebrate the cosmic Christ incarnate in the body of Jesus of Nazareth. In celebrating the birth of the Christ as historical event, as cosmic event in time, we also celebrate it as present event, as transformation of now and tomorrow. "This birth is always happening," said Meister Eckhart. "And yet, if it does not occur in me, how could it help me? Everything depends on that."[22]

---

[22] Raymond Bernard Blakeny, trans., *Meister Eckhart: A Modern Translation*, (New York: Harper and Brothers, 1941), p. 95.

CHRISTMAS DAY

Torah	Genesis 21:1–7[23]
Writing	1 Corinthians 13[23]
Prophet	Proverbs 8:1–11
Gospel	Luke 2:(1–7) 8–20

Given the dominance of the traditional Christmas gospel story from Luke for both Christmas Eve and Christmas Day, one is a little hard pressed to seek out other scriptures. What might they say – indeed, what *can* they say – in light of the greater story of the birth of Jesus?

The texts I have chosen for today are present to help begin a celebration of the *via positiva* and at the same time explore aspects of the newborn Christ child.

The reading from Genesis tells of the birth of Isaac, child of the promise made to Abraham and Sarah in their old age. The joy surrounding this birth is a strong parallel to the joy at the birth of Jesus. At the same time, the story of this elderly couple achieving a child so late in life speaks to the fact that God's miracles did not begin with Jesus. That God loves children seems clear in the plethora of stories regarding special births throughout the scripture. Here, Sarah declares that this child has brought her laughter, and indeed upon hearing the story all the world will laugh with her.

1 Corinthians 13 is undoubtedly one of the most familiar and popular passages of scripture, often read at weddings. Such is a bit of a shame, because the passage then gets caught up in thoughts of romance, whereas the passage is more profound.

Verse 11 is noteworthy because of its traditional interpretation. This is most often seen as the author (Paul) stating he is glad to be rid of the things of childhood. Yet is that really what it says? It can also be understood as Paul lamenting the loss of childhood innocence; perhaps a stronger reading might be "You know, when I was a child, I had a child's imagination, and wonder, and

---

[23] Both of these stories – "Sarah's Laughter" and "Dare to Love" – can be found in paraphrased form in my book *Bible Wonderings: Familiar Tales Retold* (Lincoln, NB: iUniverse, 2006).

amazement at the things of the world. Sadly, as I grew older, I cast all this aside. More's the pity, really – I wish I still had some of that child-like zeal and wonder as I try to tackle today's strange questions."

The Proverbs reading brings us the voice of Wisdom, calling from the city gates and the street corners. As she calls us to a new awareness of justice and how to live as citizens of God's realm she provides a foretaste to the child Jesus, crying even from the manger to challenge the powers and authorities of his world.

The last reading from Luke is either a continuation of the text from last night, or a repetition. Either is most appropriate – it never hurts to hear a story more than once, and it can also be helpful to break it up. In this way we might celebrate the birth of the Christ, and also celebrate the rather distinct second part of the story which tells about the world's (shepherds') first reaction to the good news.

CHRISTMAS 1

Torah	1 Samuel 3:1–10
Writing	Isaiah 49:13–18
Prophet	Luke 2:29–38
Gospel	Luke 2:41–52

As is a common tradition for this Sunday, the story of the young Jesus teaching in the Temple is included, juxtaposed with the call of the prophet Samuel to reinforce the theme of God's interest in the ministry of children and youth. Likewise, in keeping with a general celebration of children, the Writing is a poetic selection from Isaiah portraying God as a mother who cannot forget her children.

The prophets who speak this week are Simeon and Anna, even though the actual words of the latter have not been preserved.

In the Torah reading God calls a child to prophetic ministry and an elder in the community recognizes this gift – a strong parallel to the texts from Luke.

This is one of those weeks where I will readily grant that the labeling of the various passages seems extremely arbitrary. Yet, on the other hand, there is an important challenge within that very act of labeling, to see certain texts within different lights. Simeon and Anna are clearly prophets, and the poetic text from Isaiah is as worthy a psalm as any that are so labeled. The use of 1 Samuel as "Torah" is certainly questionable. However, its importance as a text to parallel Luke 2 seemed to justify its inclusion.

EPIPHANY

Torah	Deuteronomy 10:12–22
Writing	1 Corinthians 2:6–13
Prophet	1 Kings 19:1–4, 8–15a
Gospel	Matthew 2:1–12

The Epiphany story is proclaimed in the traditional narrative from Matthew. However, the other texts expound on how God is revealed in our presence: a text from Deuteronomy speaks of us seeing God with our own eyes through God's compassion to foreigners, orphans, and widows. The prophetic text recounts Elijah's encounter with God in the proverbial still small voice – or the "sound of sheer silence" as the *New Revised Standard Version* puts it.

1 Corinthians 2:6–13 (the writing this week) is one of the New Testament texts wherein Jesus is equated with Sophia/Wisdom. Within this context the text serves well to complement Matthew's story of Christ being recognized by those of another place, by those on the outside. To quote Susan Cady, et al:

> But still we have a Sophia to offer those who have reached maturity: not a philosophy of our age, it is true, still less of the masters of our age, which are coming to their end. The hidden Sophia of God that we teach in our mysteries is the Sophia that God predestined to be for our glory before the ages began. She is a Sophia that none of the masters of this age have ever known.[24]

---

[24] 1 Corinthians 2:6–8, from Susan Cady, Marian Ronan, Hal Taussig, *Wisdom's Feast: Sophia in Study and Celebration*, (San Francisco: Harper and Row, 1989), p. 33.

Season after the Epiphany/Ordinary Time

Some notes on the season:

- For this season I have arbitrarily chosen to provide regular lections for seven weeks, recognizing that the season can frequently be longer or shorter, depending on the date of Easter.

- I have included two optional weeks (weeks 7 and 8) that are "lifted" in from the season of Transformation; these can be used on the years when Epiphany has more than seven weeks.

- Use the appropriate number of weeks, including "Last Sunday after Epiphany" on the last Sunday of this season.

- For the Sundays after the Epiphany, I have employed a parallel reading pattern (not unlike the Revised Common Lectionary in the Season after Pentecost) from Torah and the Gospel. These provide stories about our Hebrew ancestors in the former, and stories about Jesus in the latter. Readings from the Psalms (and one from Song of Solomon) as well as the prophets round out the readings.

- I have not included the traditional observances of the Baptism of Jesus and Transfiguration in keeping with a desire to focus on themes of Creation Spirituality rather than the so-called "lesser" festivals of the church year (see Chapter 2).

1ST AFTER THE EPIPHANY

Torah	Genesis 12:1–9
Writing	Psalm 99
Prophet	Isaiah 35:1–10
Gospel	John 1:(1–5), 6–18

The first reading recounts the call of Abram and Sarai to leave all that is known and familiar and trust God in a new adventure. This is *via positiva*, in the awareness of the presence of God in the call, in the journey, and in both the place of origin and in the destination.

Psalm 99 celebrates the attributes of God as one who forgives, who loves and establishes justice and righteousness, and calls us to do the same. These are key elements of the *via positiva*, firmly grounding us in an awareness of God as lover of justice – and of us. This is the God of original blessing, not of original sin. This is the God who makes deserts bloom, as Isaiah attests.

This is also the God of the cosmic Christ, glorified in John's prologue. We read the first portion in Advent, and read the conclusion today (with the option of reading the first part again).

One of the powerful truths of this text from John – and which in turn makes this a powerful witness for Creation Spirituality – is the fact that it speaks of the cosmic Christ fully incarnate in a Jesus who is completely present in our world. He "pitched his tent among us" (verse 14) and lived among us, living, breathing, eating, crying, going to the toilet, laughing, and knowing our life. At the same time he was/is divine. Amazing stuff.

2ND AFTER THE EPIPHANY

Torah	Genesis 15:1–6
Writing	Psalm 139:1–18
Prophet	Isaiah 42:1–9
Gospel	John 1:43–50

The story of Abram and Sarai continues with the promise of descendants as many as the stars of the sky, and a relationship between Abram and God that is built on trust. Psalm 139 celebrates God knowing us intimately and deeply. Just as God knows all of the stars, so God knows every cell of our being. More images of God as lover of justice are presented, this time in the first servant song from Isaiah.

The gospel reading is a traditional one for this season, and finds a place still in this lectionary. Jesus calls Philip, who in turn calls Nathanael. It is a story of beginnings of Jesus' ministry, and a delightful suggestion of a sense of humor on the part of Jesus in verse 50. ("You believe because of what I told you? Boy, are you in for surprises!") One could conclude the reading with verse 51, which I will admit is logical, but there is a certain strength in the story by ending at verse 50.

3RD AFTER THE EPIPHANY

Torah	Exodus 26:30–36
Writing	Psalm 100
Prophet	Nehemiah 8:1–3, 5–6, 8–10
Gospel	John 6:1–15

The reading from Exodus may at first seem obscure. However, in its specific and detailed description of the care one should take of the tabernacle – sign of the presence of God in the midst of the people – it is a wonderful text for the *via positiva*. This is paired with Psalm 100, a brilliant celebration of God's presence.

The reading from Nehemiah appears in the Roman and Revised Common lectionaries on this same week in Year C. Including it here in this lectionary was not completely intentional, but simply seemed a logical fit. Both this text and the one from John's gospel speak of inclusion of all in community. In the former case, the people come home and reconnect with their culture and homeland through the hearing of their story in their own language. Hearing it interpreted leads them into action of sharing.

In the gospel there is again connection with heritage and story (Passover) and a story of feeding. Furthermore in this version of the familiar feeding of the multitude story the involvement of a child as a pivotal character.

Children are not peripheral in God's realm, they are essential. They are more than simply a convenient means of transitioning from infancy to adulthood, little entities that are to be "seen and not heard," but rather teachers and leaders and prophets. God comes as a child. God calls children. They are a gift, a celebration, a wondrous part of the *via positiva*.

4TH AFTER THE EPIPHANY

Torah	Genesis 21:9–21
Writing	Psalm 27
Prophet	Isaiah 11:1–9
Gospel	John 6:35–40

The story of Hagar and Ishmael is a *via positiva* text in that it is a profound story of God hearing the voice of the rejected, of the one who has been marginalized by the official story. The fact that the story is told is powerful by and of itself.

This is a story of God's compassion which is the very essence of God. The reality of God not giving up on us, and not rejecting us once and for all in that legendary garden, is evidence that God will not abandon. And if God will not abandon us, then God is bound (literally) to join with us in suffering, in our journey. Such is compassion.

This is supported by Psalm 27 ("even if my mother and father reject me, God will be with me") and also by John 6:35–40. Jesus' offering of himself as bread is a powerful image of compassion. Beyond that, Jesus as bread is here for the salvation of all persons.

The image of Jesus offering himself as bread works for the *via negativa* as well, but it feels important to explore that image in the context of the *via positiva*, in terms of Jesus' self-understanding as one who is present to serve, to feed, to be a source of life.

The choice of Isaiah 11, traditionally an Advent text, brings hope into the equation, and takes away the direct use of this text as a prediction of Jesus. It reminds us of God's compassion for creation and for bringing justice and harmony within the creation with the juxtaposition of former enemies – perhaps in anticipation of the descendants of Ishmael and Isaac eventually reconciling?

5TH AFTER THE EPIPHANY

(Omit in 2013 and 2016. In 2018 you may omit it if you celebrated the Epiphany on January 7.)

Torah	Numbers 9:15–23
Writing	Psalm 30
Prophet	Isaiah 30:18–26
Gospel	Luke 12:22–32

God leads the people of Israel by day and by night. Just as God does not abandon them, so God does not abandon us. God turns our mourning into dancing, our sorrow into joy. God cares for our deepest needs. Above all else, God is the very essence of justice.

The choice of the Lucan passage over its parallel from Matthew 6:25-34 was a bit of a tossup, frankly. Whereas unique to Matthew is the admonition to seek God's righteousness in addition to God's realm (verse 33), Luke includes in verse 32 the statement that "it has pleased your Abba to give you the kindom" (The Inclusive Bible), and this latter seemed more in keeping with the *via positiva*. Further, the Luke text is a stronger complement to Isaiah 30:18–26 and its emphasis on God's desire to grant justice, which is such a powerful theme throughout scripture, especially the Hebrew scriptures.

It needs to be emphasized in this season as we seek to establish the *via positiva* and the concept of original blessing. "Divine justice involved [God] being merciful, compassionate," states Jewish scholar and mystic Abraham Joshua Heschel, in reference to this passage.[25] He continues, "Justice dies when dehumanized, no matter how exactly it may be exercised. Justice dies when deified, for beyond all justice is God's compassion. The logic of justice may seem impersonal, yet the concern for justice is an act of love." This is the God who clothes us, and feeds us, as God did once upon a time in Eden.

---

[25] Abraham Heschel, *The Prophets,* (New York: Harper Collins, 2001), p. 257.

6TH AFTER THE EPIPHANY

(Omit in 2010, 2013, 2016, and 2018.)

Torah	Numbers 15:22–29
Writing	Song of Songs 2:8–13
Prophet	Romans 7:15–25a
Gospel	John 4:5–42

The gospel reading this week comes from John, the story of Jesus and the Samaritan woman at the well. How is this a *via positiva* story? Jesus unequivocally and unashamedly affirms the woman's personhood. He talks to her, invites her to serve him, offers her living water, and does not judge her.

Yet beyond this, it is a *via positiva* story for the woman's witness, for the willingness of her community to listen to her, and in turn for the very ministry to the Samaritans themselves. It is a story of the affirmation of life.

This gets beautifully complemented by the reading from the Song of Songs, itself a pure and simple celebration of life. Love, life, beauty are all to be appreciated with the senses, and celebrated. This is God's world. It is a good thing. How would we dare think differently?

This sets the stage for encountering the story – yes, story – that appears in the passage from Romans. When we see this as profound theological discourse we miss, ironically, the theology of the piece.

This is Paul at his raw and honest rabbinic best. He makes neither excuse nor alibi, but simply states the reality to which we can all relate: "this is how I feel. I get up in the morning with good intentions, and then I procrastinate. God, please, enter and bail me out. It's not that I'm wicked, or filthy, or wrong, or bad, it's just that I have these moments. And in these moments, I need to be transformed. I need breakthrough. I need to embrace my *via negativa* and return to the *via positiva* that is the core of my essential being."

Paul is not saying "I am original sin" but rather "I have clouded my original blessing because I am human. It's the way it goes. I don't like it. God, help me."

This in turn is complemented by the reading from Numbers in which is revealed, somewhat hidden in the details of legal code, the compassion of God. Even within the confines of the sacrificial system with its myriad rules and technicalities, provision is made to cover those – both Jew and gentile – who might sin unintentionally.

7TH AFTER THE EPIPHANY

(For use in 2011, 2014, 2017, and 2019. These same lections also appear on Transformativa 19.)

Torah	Matthew 5:1–12 *or* Luke 6:20–23 (24–26)
Writings	Psalm 19
Prophet	Ezekiel 37:1–14
Gospel	John 2:1–12[26]

This week the Torah readings are the beatitudes. At the outset we must readily concede that there are substantial differences between Matthew's beatitudes and Luke's, but I nonetheless offer the two as options. This allows you to choose according to your desired emphasis.

Various translations render the opening word of the beatitudes in a variety of ways, generally either "blessed" or "happy" and, in the case of the second half of the Lucan version, either "woe to you" or "cursed are you." The Jesus Seminar gave a red rating (indicating they are probably Jesus' genuine words) to much of the first part of Luke's text, rendering them "Congratulations, you poor!" etc. They gave a black rating (extremely unlikely to be the words of Jesus) to the second half, which they rendered "Damn you rich!" etc.[27]

Neil Douglas-Klotz has done ground-breaking work seeking to reconstruct the sayings of Jesus in the original Aramaic. He has offered a variety of renderings of Matthew's beatitudes, using such introductory words as "Happy and aligned with the One are those who…" and "Tuned to the Source…" and "Healed are those who…"[28] Such concepts take the text out of the "religious" realm and make it more accessible and, I believe, more transforming.

The portion of the Luke passage (verses 24-26) that contain the "woes" may not seem appropriate for the *via positiva* and thus could

---

[26] For a retelling of this story in a modern setting see "After the Wedding" in my book *Bible Wonderings*.

[27] Robert W. Funk, Roy W. Hoover, and the Jesus Seminar, *The Five Gospels: the Search for the Authentic Words of Jesus*, (New York: MacMillan, 1993), p. 289.

[28] Neil Douglas-Klotz, *Prayers of the Cosmos: Meditations on the Aramaic Words of Jesus*, (San Francisco: Harper, 1990), p. 47.

be omitted. However, leaving them in reminds us that even within this path there is balance between "good and evil." There can be something positive about confronting and even embracing the polar opposite of righteous living.

The other readings all contain various elements of the *via positiva:* the heavens declare God's praise to the ends of the earth, yet without sound; dead bones come to life; water becomes wine. Yet even within these texts are sub-themes that challenge some of our preconceptions and sensibilities as well.

Psalm 19 celebrates God's "law" (always a dismal translation of *torah*) and thus challenges those of us who are preconditioned to think of law – or even of the Hebrew scriptures – as rigid legalism to be avoided at all costs. Instead we are invited to remember that *torah* is not law in our twenty-first century, courtroom understanding, but God's liberating way. It can in fact be described and celebrated as something "sweeter than honey."

The story of the wedding at Cana challenges us with the image of a God who sees life as a celebration, and who wants the celebration to continue. We have an image of Jesus being reluctant to leap into ministry. We also have an image of Mary taking the initiative in ministry.

All in all, an exciting wondering of the *via positiva.*

8TH AFTER THE EPIPHANY

(For use in 2011. These same lections also appear on Transformativa 22.)

Torah	Matthew 5:21–24
Writings	Galatians 2:(15–18) 19–21
Prophet	2 Samuel 6:1–5, 12–19
Gospel	Mark 5:25–34

In this portion of the Sermon on the Mount, Jesus seeks to expand our understanding of the Law. More than technicalities, it is our intent that matters. Intent is the key to the woman's actions in the story from Mark as well.

Without making any fuss, she seeks to touch Jesus' cloak quietly and discreetly, believing that this can somehow change her situation. Jesus, in turn, is intent on giving her more: naming her ("Daughter") and proclaiming her healed.

The Prophet text tells of David bringing the ark into Jerusalem, with the ensuing celebration that includes dancing, merriment, and the sharing of food. (Following the lead of other lectionaries, I have left out the portion that deals with the death of Uzzah.)

In Galatians we read of Paul's explanation of justification by grace. Marcus Borg points out that this text, like much of Paul's writing, does not feed into the "Jesus died for my sins because I was a bad person" explanation. Rather it speaks to the the understanding of Christ's death as showing the way to God, as "the embodiment or incarnation of the path of internal psychological and spiritual transformation that lies at the center of the Christian life."[29]

We celebrate the entry into the new Jerusalem, the new life, and the new realities to which Christ leads us.

---

[29] Borg, *Heart of Christianity*, p. 93.

LAST SUNDAY AFTER THE EPIPHANY

Torah	Numbers 35:9–15
Writing	Psalm 126
Prophet	Jeremiah 33:1–11
Gospel	Mark 4:35–41

The instruction on establishing cities of refuge from Numbers seems a logical place to close off this season. As we have read some of the key passages establishing God's initial relationship with creation (including humankind), it is worth noting God's compassion extending to those who have made mistakes. The compassion here is both exceptional and explicit: a total of six cities of refuge, to welcome Israelite and foreigner. God's compassion does not recognize boundaries.

This text is complemented with Psalm 126's rejoicing over the harvest, and Jeremiah's foretelling of a day of shouts of gladness and joy one day at the restoration of the people, based on his assurance of the steadfastness of God's eternal love. The gospel reading attests to this same love in the story of Jesus calming a storm in the presence of the disciples.

In the case of this last, I chose Mark's version because of the disciples' question – "Teacher, don't you care if we perish?" – and Jesus' words to the storm, "Peace, be still!" There seems in both of these statements much opportunity for conversation around the presence of God in our questions, in our assumptions, in the word of God, and in the presence of Christ.

The doubting of the disciples here is not a criticism of them, but simply an awareness for them – and for us – that doubt is a part of the faith process, part of the growth process. "Imperfection is not a sign of the absence of God," declares Matthew Fox. "It is a sign that the ongoing creation is no easy thing. We all bear scars from this rugged process. We can – and must – celebrate the scars."[30]

This, in turn, leads us directly into the *via negativa.*

---

[30] Fox, *Original Blessing,* pp. 110–111.

Chapter 6 – *Via Negativa:* Lent

In many traditions, Lent has been a season of giving up – but giving up in terms of suffering, of taking on guilt, of contemplating our unworthiness, our sinfulness. If ever there was a season where fall/redemption theology shone, this was it.

But what if Lent becomes a time in which we explore the *via negativa?* What if in this season we are provided an opportunity to meet our negative side not as something bad that must be rejected, but as something that can be embraced and offered to God?

The "Torah" readings for the Sundays during Lent follow the story of David, and in so doing invite us to confront pain, sin, difficulty, and darkness. It is only by confronting these things that we can truly confront the complete reality of who we are, who we have become, and who we can yet be.

The other scriptures have been chosen to support these stories, to guide one in a season of pouring out, and spending time in an awareness of sin – not in terms of breast-beating guilt but rather as that state of being in which we are distanced from our creator and long for reconnection. This in turn sets us up, hopefully, for Easter as the ultimate moment of breakthrough – of experiencing the *via creativa.*

ASH WEDNESDAY

Torah	Joshua 24:14–18
Writing	Romans 3:19–26
Prophet	Isaiah 58
Gospel	Luke 7:36–50

As the season begins, we transition from *via positiva* to *via negativa*. We begin a time of letting go, a season of making choices.

We begin with Joshua's challenge to the people of Israel and ask ourselves, "can we let go of our old gods and choose God?" Indeed, in many ways Joshua's question was given new voice by Meister Eckhart when he said, "God does not ask anything else of you except that you let yourself go and let God be God in you."[31] This is what it is to choose God.

The prophet Isaiah confronts us in a similar way. Isaiah 58 (found in the Revised Common Lectionary as an optional first reading for this day) challenges us to confess with integrity. Like other prophets, the one generally known as second Isaiah issues a call for a practical fast: "Remove the chains of oppression and the yoke of injustice, and let the oppressed go free. Share your food with the hungry and open your homes to the homeless poor. Give clothes to those who have nothing to wear…" (Isaiah 58:6b–7a, TEV). This awareness of sin is reiterated in Romans 3:23: "Everyone has sinned; everyone falls short of the glory of God" (Inclusive Bible). Yet, while fall/redemption theologians would stop there – and many fundamentalist Christians do, especially during Lent – we read the next part: "Yet everyone has also been undeservedly justified by the gift of God" (verse 24).

The sacrificial imagery in this passage has led to an emphasis on Jesus as sacrificial lamb of God without examining the context of the Temple cult and the way in which those who were steeped in that tradition might have more readily understood this death. Marcus Borg addresses this beautifully in *The Heart of Christianity:*

> The metaphor of sacrifice…subverted the sacrificial system. It meant: God in Jesus has already provided the sacrifice

---

[31] Matthew Fox, *Meditations with Meister Eckhart*, (Santa Fe: Bear and Co., 1982), p. 52.

and has thus taken care of whatever you think separates you from God; you have access to God apart from the temple and its system of sacrifice. It is a metaphor of radical grace, of amazing grace.

Thus "Jesus died for our sins" was originally a subversive metaphor, not a literal description of either God's purpose or Jesus' vocation. It was a metaphorical proclamation of radical grace; and properly understood, it still is.[32]

Such an understanding is crucial so as not to fall into a more classical trap of understanding this in terms of "I am so bad God had no choice but to kill Jesus." This implication that God is somehow tied by rules of God's own making is naïve at best. Furthermore, God has repeatedly rejected the sacrificial cult according to the prophets (see Isaiah 1:11–14, Hosea 6:6, and Amos 5:1–24, to name only a few examples). To suggest that our behavior forces God to act in a certain way implies that we are more powerful than God, a notion that is not supported in scripture.[33]

The gospel reading is the story of the woman anointing Jesus while he is at the home of Simon the Pharisee – a profound story of pouring out, and awareness of forgiveness. Beyond this, it is a reminder that the community of Jesus is of the proverbial "lowest of the low," the ones who are seen at the edges of society. In this story Jesus asserts that all are welcome.

Elisabeth Schüssler Fiorenza suggests that this was seen as a baptismal story in the early church, and further sees it as affirmation that "the notion of atoning sacrifice does not express the Jesus movement's understanding and experience of God but is a later interpretation of the violent death of Jesus in cultic terms. The God of Jesus is not a God who demands atonement…"[34] This helps support a Creation Spirituality reading of Romans 3:19–26.

---

[32] Borg, *Heart of Christianity*, p. 95.

[33] Nor anywhere else, I should dare to think!

[34] Elisabeth Schüssler Fiorenza, *In Memory of Her: a Feminist Theological Reconstruction of Christian Origins*, (New York: Crossroad, 1985), p. 130.

In the context of God's grace and the challenge to do justice, we can move into a time of pouring out all that we are and have been, and confront the *via negativa*.

LENT 1

Torah	1 Samuel 16:1–13
Writing	Psalm 90
Prophet	Joel 2:1a, 12–16
Gospel	Mark 1:14–15

From the earliest days, the season of Lent has begun with a reading of the story of Jesus' temptation in the wilderness, as this story attempts to give a biblical context for the season of Lent. Yet the parallel is somewhat false: the biblical reference is undoubtedly not to a literal 40 days, nor is Lent exactly 40 days. Beyond that we are not beginning our ministry, as Jesus was, nor are we facing the realities that Jesus was facing.

Furthermore, however, the reading of that story grounds the season ever more fully in fall/redemption theology and the sense of temptation to sin and the need to be rescued from that. Accordingly it seems important to move away from that tradition, and instead to begin the season with Jesus' call to repentance.

In so doing, it pays to remember that the biblical meaning of "repent" is to "turn around." We turn away from sin, yes, but even more importantly we turn – or return – to God. Rather than journey into the wilderness, we journey from it in the *via negativa*. We recognize that we are there, that the wilderness, the darkness, is a part of our life already. Not to be feared, nor to be avoided, but to be recognized, and journeyed through. When we repent, we return from exile to our true home, which is in God.

As we repent and start again, we read the story of Samuel moving through his own time of *via negativa* to anoint young David as the future ruler. A lament psalm, and the traditional Lenten reading from the prophet Joel (usually read at Ash Wednesday) round out the readings for this first Sunday.

LENT 2

Torah	1 Samuel 17:(12–20), 21–40, (41–49)
Writing	Psalm 102
Prophet	Amos 7:10–15
Gospel	Luke 4:10–13

The key here is to focus on the power of God to challenge our own sense of power, and thus one can use the longer or the shorter story from 1 Samuel. The reality is that there is violence in the world, and so we can be up front about it and include the story of the death of Goliath, without glorifying it. I believe the story can be told without the sense of "God is on our side." However, a powerful enough story can be had simply by focusing on the central portion where, despite rejection from those who would judge on appearances, David presents himself as an agent of God. Being so chosen he also rejects the weaponry of the world, deliberately facing great danger armed only with alternative sources of strength and spiritual might.

The reading from Amos echoes some of the sentiments of the first reading, with Amos protesting his "innocence" as it were in terms of the role in which he has found himself. He had not planned to be a prophet, to speak the word of truth so plainly, but it was God's doing. Psalm 102 has been chosen to complement these two readings.

For the gospel, we read the story of Jesus' temptation – the story that traditionally is read on the first Sunday of Lent. Here Jesus, like David, is faced with fear and temptation, embodied in one called The Adversary or, in Greek the *satan*. The word often gets turned into a proper name, but it really is best understood in the way we would use the term "devil's advocate." This entity embodies the very antithesis of God, and challenges – in much the same way that Goliath does with David – Jesus to abandon his true self and give in to fear, hunger, lust for power. Yet, like David, emboldened by the Spirit of God, Jesus lets go the powers and temptations and fears of the world and in so doing maintains integrity and defeats evil.

This links with David's and Amos' trust in God, and reminds us of the need to be open, to bare ourselves to God if we are to be born again, if we are to be agents of rebirth. Eckhart writes, "For God wishes to have, and has to have, an unencumbered, untroubled, and free soul for this birth, a soul in which there is nothing but him alone, a soul that looks out for nothing and no one but for him alone."[35]

---

[35] Sermon 18, in Fox, *Passion for Creation*, p. 255.

LENT 3

Torah	1 Samuel 18:1–9
Writing	2 Samuel 1:17–27
Prophet	Amos 2:10–12
Gospel	Mark 3:(20–30), 31–35

This week both the Torah and writing passages come from the David saga. We read of the love between David and Jonathan, and of the source of Saul's jealousy of David, and then read of the lament and the hymn that David sings for both of them – one his friend (and possibly his lover), the other his former mentor and later sworn enemy.

This example of whom we dare to love, and mourn, is reinforced in Jesus' pronouncement about his true family in Mark 3:31–35. The earlier passage about Jesus being confronted on the source of his power, and his explanation regarding same, can be included or not, depending on the theme you wish to emphasize.

The short reading from Amos, almost in the form of lament, forms what Abraham Heschel described as "the utterance of a Redeemer who is pained by the misdeeds, the thanklessness of those whom He has redeemed."[36] All in all, a mood of pain and sadness hovers over this Lenten day. A light is relentlessly shined into our places of recognition in these stories.

---

[36] Heschel, *The Prophets*, p. 39.

LENT 4

Torah	2 Samuel 11:1–27 (12:1–7a)
Writing	Psalm 51
Prophet	Amos 5:10–15
Gospel	Luke 23:26–31

The introduction to Psalm 51 says that David wrote it after the prophet Nathan confronted him with the truth of his affair with Bathsheba and its aftermath, and certainly the texts belong together.

This is such a multi-faceted story: the dehumanizing by David of first Bathsheba (turning her into a plaything) and then Uriah (turning him into an obstacle to be removed) presents an important aspect of sin. David's fanatical desire to cover his tracks at any cost is another angle. The contrast between Uriah's loyalty to his comrades and David's lack thereof is another. Finally, David's righteous indignation at the parable Nathan tells him (not actually in these readings, but referred to in the Psalm) is yet another piece.

Reading Psalm 51 in the context of its story and setting places verse 5 in its appropriate context and diffuses it as a proof–text for the concept of original sin. The expression "I was born guilty, a sinner when my mother conceived me" (NRSV) is not a systematic declaration but the rhetorical claim of someone who is pleading for mercy. "Hear me out, God. I cannot help it. I was born this way. Give me another chance." Have not each of us, in times of angst or despair, cried out in similar rhetoric? This is hardly a profound theological pronouncement, but simply a real and momentary thought.

The gospel text, taken from Luke's passion narrative, includes Jesus' lament for Jerusalem. The passage from Amos describes desperate and dismal times, but contains a glimmer of hope. There is light at the end of the tunnel. There is dawn after the darkest of nights. There is an empty tomb beyond the cross. Yet for now we confront the truths of the nighttime.

LENT 5

Torah	2 Samuel 12:15b–23
Writing	Psalm 137
Prophet	Amos 8:1–12
Gospel	Luke 8:49–56

There are numerous stories of David that are, by necessity, not able to be included in this Lenten journey through the *via negativa*. We conclude the story of David with the story of the death of David and Bathsheba's child. The amazing honesty with which David accepts the child's death shows us the embrace of darkness that the *via negativa* teaches us is so essential.

In addressing this text it will be helpful not to ignore the fact that this story suggests the death of the child was God's will. The point can be raised forthright, and then one can point out that this speaks of a common misunderstanding in David's time, and no longer the way we see things. There is nothing wrong with confronting such passages of scripture – indeed, they provide excellent opportunities for reminding ourselves that the Bible is an ancient book and its stories are to be read in their historic context.

Psalm 137 could be described as the quintessential *via negativa* psalm. Indeed, to confront its presence in the canon – or at least verses 8 and 9 – and embrace the pain and difficulty they connote can be by and of itself an experience of the *via negativa*. Yet confront them we must, for they are a genuine sentiment, the cry of one who has suffered injustice and experienced first hand that all is not right with the world.

It can be risky – even downright dangerous – to read a text like Psalm 137 in an era of racial and inter-religious violence. There is no doubt that it is inflammatory. But it is also real.

Such a psalm reminds us of our sacred right, and duty, to be perfectly honest with God when we are in prayer. It does not invite us to curse others, or invoke God's wrath, but to confront our honest feelings and share them with God, that we might throw them in the fire and so create warmth and light that could even be shared with those we might formerly have named as enemies.

It is a text that reminds us of the need for lament, of the need to utter our true pain from the depths of the soul, that it might not fester but find full expression. This is one of the gifts of the *via negativa*, that we can pour out such grief and pain and even anger, secure in the knowledge that God not only forgives us but, when we are honest and open, prevents us from bringing such feelings to full fruition before it is too late.

Along with this psalm we read a passage without hope from Amos, and this in turn is balanced with one of sheer hope and amazement from Luke. Jesus dares to confront a group of mourners, incurs their derision, touches a dead body, "wastes" his time with a non-person (female child) and does what he does best: restores life, and affirms personhood.

PALM/PASSION SUNDAY

| *Gospel* | Luke 19:28–40 *(Liturgy of the Palms)* |
| *Gospel* | Luke 22:14 – 23:56 *(Liturgy of the Passion)* |

There are always difficulties using readings from the Hebrew scriptures during Holy Week, given the tragic history of anti–Judaism and anti–Semitism in the history of the Christian church, as well as the sensitivity with which one must approach the whole issue about reading the life of Christ back into the Hebrew scriptures, as it were. Accordingly, I have intentionally chosen only passages from the gospels for Holy Week, letting the story speak for itself. The next question is, of course, which gospel? The choice is extremely arbitrary.

I have defaulted to Luke for this first reading of the passion narrative, finding in it less of the anti-Semitism of John, the proof-texting (and inherent anti-Semitism) of Matthew, and yet also finding it a bit richer and fuller than Mark. Whichever one chooses, however, it is vital to remember that we are dealing here with *story*. We can get too hung up on the precision of the vessel that contains the story (in other words, the particulars of the text) that we lose the story itself. The conflict of the powers, the challenge to political and religious authority, the turning of the crowds, the willingness of Jesus to stop at nothing to demonstrate God's love, the power of forgiveness, the testimony of the women, the agony of Christ's suffering and death are only a few pieces that are present here.

The reading for the Palm liturgy is also from Luke, largely for continuity's sake (although in so doing we also avoid Matthew's confusing inclusion of two donkeys) and also includes the wonderful connection with the created world in Jesus' admonition that, were the crowds to be silenced, the stones themselves would shout.

Amongst all of the various aspects of "who do we blame" for the death of Jesus, Bruce Chilton makes an intriguing point in his biography of Jesus.

> Time and again, the Gospels reveal the tendency of the first Christians to shift the blame for Jesus' death away from Pilate and onto the Sanhedrin. Yet when it comes to taking on the weighty responsibility of burying Jesus, we find

members of that same council taking the lead, while most of Jesus' disciples had beaten a hasty and ignominious retreat. Joseph's and Nicodemus' public act cost them: they donated mortuary dressing and ointment as well as use of the cave. They also contracted uncleanness for seven days after the burial.[37]

As there is no room in Creation Spirituality for any exclusion, there is especially no room for anti-Semitism; any opportunities that the scriptures provide to challenge the anti-Semitism that we may find (or that some may search for, to support their own biases) should be taken.

---

[37] Bruce Chilton, *Rabbi Jesus: an Intimate Biography*, (New York: Doubleday, 2000), p. 270.

MAUNDY/HOLY THURSDAY

Gospel   Mark 14:12–50 (51–52)

For the re-enactment of Holy Week events, I have chosen Mark – by default again, rejecting Matthew and John for the reasons given on Palm/Passion Sunday, and having already used Luke.

This reading follows essentially the events of Thursday night, according to Mark: Jesus' Passover meal with his disciples (beginning with its preparations), the conversation with Peter, prayer in Gethsemane, and arrest. The reason for leaving verses 51–52 as an option is that, on the one hand there is really no reason to exclude them, and they belong here rather than with the latter portion to be read on Good Friday but, on the other hand, there is something very powerful in ending this day's reading with the statement "Then all the disciples left him and ran away" (Mark 14:50, *Good News Bible*).

GOOD FRIDAY

Gospel   Mark 14:53 – 15:47

This reading simply continues on from Maundy Thursday through the trial, crucifixion, death, and burial of Jesus.

EASTER VIGIL

My initial thought was not to include readings for an Easter vigil. The "mini-lectionary" that makes up the traditional readings for this day seems intent on showing that all of biblical history was pointing to the life, death, and resurrection of Jesus, and this is hardly in keeping with the understandings of Creation Spirituality. But the challenge then became not to reject the observance because of this potential for theological misuse, but instead to reshape it within the four paths.

Accordingly, after contemplation and struggle my proposal is for a series of eight readings. Any attempt to try and work with the other construct of Torah, Writing, Prophet, and Gospel seemed too unwieldy, artificial and – frankly – overwhelming, as it would presumably have led to sixteen scripture passages. So, there are simply two readings for each of the four paths, without any regard to the "source" of the various readings.

One might choose to read them in their couplets, or in a series of two cycles, or even randomly. Alternatively one might read them randomly, providing the worshiper with the opportunity to form their own journey as a floating, fluid thing. This avoids imposing a strict theological understanding and interpretation on the choice of texts themselves.

In this interlude between crucifixion and resurrection, perhaps more so than at any other time of the year, it feels quite uncomfortable to impose lectionary "weight" upon anyone. I realize that saying that seems a bit ludicrous – this is a lectionary, after all. Yet, by offering the texts with optional suggestions for their use and order, there is more room for them to stand on their own.

Via Positiva:	John 14:1–4
	Psalm 106
Via Negativa	Malachi 2:17 – 3:5
	John 12:20–26
Via Creativa	John 11:1–44
	1 Peter 2:4–10

Via Transformativa　　　　1 Thessalonians 5:1–11

　　　　　　　　　　　　　　Micah 4:1–5

Via Positiva: The John text is probably a fairly obvious choice, as we hear Jesus promising to prepare a place for us. Psalm 106 may seem a bit more obscure, but it is a good grounding in the basic tenets of our faith. God's love and wrath are at the beginning and ending of this psalm, with justice in the middle. Love and wrath are the two sides of a coin, and they are joined by justice.

Via Negativa: The Malachi passage is probably familiar as an Advent text (or at least in the context of Handel's *Messiah)* and yet it fits well with the *via negativa* because of the imagery of cleansing and refining. Further, the statement about a grain of wheat needing to fall into the ground and die in order to have new life seems an obvious choice for both the *via negativa* and the transition time between Good Friday and Easter Sunday.

Via Creativa: We find breakthrough in the story of Lazarus, not simply in the obvious – the resuscitation of a dead body, and the emergence of same from a grave – but perhaps even more profoundly in the creedal statement of Martha. The passage from 1 Peter invites us to contemplate the changes inherent in recognizing ourselves as a chosen people, royal priesthood, and holy nation, as well as to contemplate the pending transformation that comes to our world and our individual lives in the transformation of earthly Jesus into cosmic Christ.

Via Transformativa: Hope, perseverance, and promise run through both of these readings, taking us full circle. The Micah passage is such a potent vision, stretching further than the parallel in Isaiah 2. Here we have not only the vision of transformation of weapons into tools for producing food, but also the image of each person sitting under their own vine and fig tree, of none being afraid, and of all the nations walking in the name of their gods. The words to the Thessalonians invite us to live as children of the light – God's light – in the brightness of the new day that dawns in Christ.

With these readings, we close the *via negativa* and prepare for the *via creativa*. As we do, we move from cross to tomb. We travel from symbol of death to place of nurture, to womb of rebirth.

As we do so, while I would not in any way suggest that we abandon the symbol of the cross, I would encourage us to embrace other symbols as well as we enter the Easter season. The early church did not use the cvross as their dominant symbol, preferring instead the fish as a symbol of the living Christ. Creation Spirituality invites us to wonder what message the cross gives when it is *the* dominant symbol, when the image presented to the world and, more importantly, to ourselves as Christians is that of suffering, of pouring out, of remaining in the *via negativa*.

The cross has its place. But are we not Easter people? Is not the resurrection of greater significance than the crucifixion?

It is no accident that the stylized cross image preferred in the west is that which closely resembles a sword. Most biblical historians will concede this image is probably not a very accurate rendition of the actual article upon which Jesus was crucified.

The tomb on the other hand is rounded, womb-like. It is neither closed nor narcissistic, but open and inviting, where one can come in and go out.

We need not fear the cross. Yet we need not fear the tomb, either. It is the tomb that releases the cross, it is the tomb that partners death, and it is the tomb that breaks through.

That Jesus died is amazing and wonderful for what it demonstrated. Yet over and against the resurrection this moment fades. At the same time it is a dominant obsession in fall/redemption theology, and in our churches today. The baptismal font is womb-shaped, but we tend to abandon that in earliest childhood, and focus on the cross ever after. It is the empty tomb, however, that as the place of God's ultimate breakthrough can provide us with new life in ways unimaginable. "Even the men who ran to the tomb, Peter and John, looked in and were amazed. But they did not stay, nor were they swallowed up by it. They moved on, very much energized. The fear of death is liberated at the tomb. For death is swallowed up in the victory."[38]

Welcome, breakthrough.

Welcome, *via creativa*.

---

[38] Fox, *Original Blessing*, p. 116.

Chapter 7 – *Via Creativa:* Easter

EASTER SUNDAY

Torah	Luke 24:1–11 *or* John 20:1–10
Writing	2 Corinthians 5:16–21
Prophet	Isaiah 65:17–25
Gospel	Luke 24:1–11 *or* John 20:1–10

"Behold, I create a new heaven and earth!" God declares (Isaiah 65:17). "If anyone is in Christ, there is a new creation, " Paul writes (2 Corinthians 5:17). This is no idle tale – Christ is risen; God has broken through. "The resurrection does not mean the rising of Jesus into the old life, but the beginning of the new creation."[39] As in the image of the caterpillar and the butterfly I mentioned earlier (p. 18), the risen Christ is more than just a resuscitated Jesus.

Two resurrection accounts are presented this morning, with the intention that both would be read: one as Torah and one as Gospel. With the John reading we begin four weeks of reading from this chapter. We begin a season of encountering the risen Christ, and exploring what that can mean. What is birthed in us with the presence of the resurrected Christ?

We read stories, and intentionally two of them that differ in details, so as to remind ourselves that the point of this is not factual history but faith history. We must not let those steeped in fall/redemption theology and conservative politics try to claim that in so doing we are diminishing the fullness of truth in these stories. To say that calling something "faith history" as opposed to "factual history" somehow diminishes its value is to denigrate faith – surely something a theologian would be very hesitant to do.

The link between the gospel accounts and the other readings is very intentional as well. They are to be read, not just as generic celebrations of "new creation" but also as specific reminders that

---

[39] Jann Aldredge-Clanton, *In Search of the Christ-Sophia: an Inclusive Christology for Liberating Christians,* (Mystic, CT: Twenty-third Publications, 1995), p. 57.

we ourselves are creators. If we are made in the image of God, who is a creator, how can we be anything else? Our creativity, too often denied, is affirmed and liberated yet again in the resurrection. It is not for the mere sake of liturgical convenience that the *via creativa* and season of Easter are merged in this lectionary; they are inextricably intertwined by divine decree, inasmuch as we are invited/nurtured/challenged to leave our tombs of self–doubt and emerge as creative beings. As Fox explains, "What happens when we apply the essence of our humanity, namely our creativity, to the Easter story? Once the fear of death – a major obstacle to creativity – is removed, can we then be free to embark on our true destiny, which is to create. To create like God does. To create for compassion's sake and celebration's sake and healing's sake and joy's sake."[40]

---

[40] Matthew Fox, *Creativity: Where the Divine and the Human Meet*, (New York: Jeremy P. Tarcher/Putnam, 2002), p. 118.

EASTER 2

Torah	Luke 15:1–10
Writing	1 John 1:5 – 2:2
Prophet	Jeremiah 31:31–34
Gospel	John 20:11–18

Throughout the remainder of the Easter season, until Pentecost Sunday, we will continue to focus on breakthrough, choosing resurrection stories as the Gospel readings for each Sunday. These will be complemented with parables serving as Torah, Writings from the epistles, and (with this week being the sole exception) stories of prophetic calls and actions.

The prologue to today's readings comes from the prophet Jeremiah, announcing a new covenant written on the heart, supported by the Writing from 1 John encouraging us to love one another. The Torah reading from Luke contains parables of God as shepherd seeking high and low for a lost sheep, and as homemaker searching every nook and cranny for a lost coin. God does not give up on us. All of this, then, sets the stage for John's version of Easter morning part 2 and the resurrection appearance to Mary Magdalene.

By separating John 20:11–18 from the first part of the chapter, we have an opportunity to put the focus of this story where it rightly belongs – on the encounter between Jesus and Mary.

This is an amazing story of breakthrough, of *via creativa* in all its resurrection power. Mary had experienced the *via positiva* through the time spent with Jesus and his proclamation of the gospel that transformed her life. In recent days, right up until this moment in the garden, she has experienced the *via negativa* in all of its fullness. Then Jesus calls her by name, and everything changes.

This links back to the "atoning sacrifice" piece in 1 John 2:2 which, at first glance – given its great popularity in the fall/redemption tradition – may seem problematic but is in fact quite liberating.

Having grown up somewhat within the Anglican tradition, I am familiar with this passage as one of the "four comfortable words" read each Sunday as part of the Eucharist liturgy, in this manner "If any man [sic] sins, we have an Advocate with the Father, Jesus Christ the righteous, and he is the propitiation for our sins." Webster's *New International Dictionary* renders "propitiate" as "to win or regain the good will of" which is a helpful translation, I think, of the Greek ιλασμος *(ilasmos)*, generally rendered "sin-offering" or, in the *NRSV* and others, "atoning sacrifice."

So what does all this mean in the context of Creation Spirituality? The fact that Jesus through his life, ministry, death, and resurrection brings us into closer relationship with God is quite clear. That he died is obvious. Was this death inevitable? Yes, if he was to remain true to proclaiming the message of unconditional love and original blessing that was his to proclaim. Was it atoning in the same way that ancient Israel understood the sacrificial cult? I'm not so sure.

In *The Heart of Christianity*, Marcus Borg gives an excellent listing of five ways that various New Testament writers understand the death of Jesus, noting that the "priestly understanding" (Jesus as sacrifice for sin, or sin-offering) in its fullest development is a rather late interpretation.[41] The idea that God would require the death of Jesus on behalf of humankind is frankly both grotesque and ludicrous: why would God make a rule that God could not break, and one so barbaric as to demand the death of God's beloved child? It defies logic. If God makes the rules, surely God can change the rules. Beyond this, God is about love, not revenge. Finally, God states on numerous occasions a preference for acts of justice over and above adherence to the sacrificial cult.

However, taken in the context of 1 John, the understanding of Jesus as sacrifice is a radical understanding of grace. Jesus' death – which proved that the power of God and the cross was/is greater than the imperial power of Rome (compare Colossians 2:17) – renders obsolete and irrelevant any notions of the need for a sacrificial system. It similarly renders obsolete even the very thought of the requisite death of Jesus, seeming oxymoron though that may be.

---

[41] Borg, *Heart of Christianity*, p. 94. The listing goes from pp. 92–94.

The death of Jesus reveals the height, breadth, and depth of God's love for us. This is atoning sacrifice. This willingness to stop at nothing to prove God's unconditional love for all creation brings us ever closer to our creator, and this is atonement (literally, "at-one-ness" or the ultimate of reconciliation). As Fox points out, "the salvation that Jesus brings is primarily liberation from the fear of death."[42] Not even that can separate us from God any more. Mary learns that in the garden; 1 John assures us that it is true for us as well.

A further advantage to separating out the story of Mary Magdalene from the earlier part of the Easter morning narrative, apart from the power of the resurrection appearance it contains, is to emphasize the apostolic ministry of Mary, that gets short enough shrift as it is, but can even more readily get buried in the shuffle of Easter Sunday lections.

It's also time to set Mary Magdalene free from the mess of legends, misunderstandings, and smear campaigns that have labeled her a prostitute, or penitent, and/or combined her with various other biblical characters. In so doing, we must at the same time recognize, celebrate, and proclaim the *via creativa* reality that happens in this story, as she is commissioned the first apostle of the risen Christ. "The traditional disparagement of Mary Magdalene highlights the radical nature of Jesus' choice of a woman as the apostle to the apostles, the one sent to bear witness of the resurrection to the male apostles. Down through the centuries the church has choked on this radically feminist act of Jesus."[43]

---

[42] Fox, *Original Blessing*, p. 168.
[43] Aldredge-Clanton, *In Search of the Christ-Sophia*, p. 40.

EASTER 3

Torah	Luke 15:11–32
Writing	1 John 3:19–24
Prophet	Jonah
Gospel	John 20:19–23

While traditionally most lectionaries have provided John 20:19–29 on the second Sunday of Easter (because of the story of Thomas encountering Jesus a week after the resurrection), my desire to give fuller attention to the various scenes within this longer narrative relegates John 20:19–23 (an Easter evening story) to this 3rd Sunday, and the Thomas story to next week.

Today's gospel, then, is another story of breakthrough – quite literally, in this case. Jesus breaks through locked doors and figuratively breaks through the disciples' fear, to breathe the Holy Spirit upon them and commission them for ministry. Sometimes referred to as John's Pentecost story, it is important to note that this commissioning of the men comes *after* the commissioning of Mary Magdalene the same morning (which we read last Sunday.)

An equally short Writing from 1 John, encouraging us to love one another, supports the short gospel reading. These two are in turn balanced out by longer readings from Torah and Prophet. In the case of the former, another parable following sequentially from last week. God is portrayed as a father who not only welcomes home a child who comes seeking forgiveness, but indeed runs to welcome that child, and spares no expense in celebrating the return, even challenging those who would question the lavishness of the celebration. Shades of this are in turn echoed by the story of the prophet Jonah.

This last is by necessity a very lengthy reading but there is no logical place to break this story and have it serve the *via creativa* adequately. In its entirety, Jonah is a wonderful story of resurrection – and not because of the allusions that Jesus makes (see Matthew 12:39–41 and parallels). Jonah's journey into *via negativa* and humorous rebirth, both from the belly of the fish and under the tree in the scorching sun, are strong affirmations of the *via creativa*.

EASTER 4

Torah	Luke 18:9–14[44]
Writing	Ephesians 2:1–10
Prophet	Acts 9:1–19
Gospel	John 20:24–29

This week's readings invite us to explore how we perceive the realities around us. Thomas needs to see in order to believe in the risen Christ, and Jesus affirms that those who need to see are blessed, and those who do not see and yet also believe are blessed as well. Paul is blinded by a light that transforms his being in every sense of the word – his physical being, and his existence. The parable of the Pharisee and the tax collector invites us to explore how we perceive ourselves, and the Ephesians text about grace culminates with the statement that Matthew Fox translates "we are God's work of art" (verse 10).[45]

This week begins a series of four Prophet readings that come from books that are not traditionally thought of as prophetic. These are chosen to continue the pattern, within the *via creativa*, of telling stories of breakthrough by exploring prophetic acts.

---

[44] For a modern-day paraphrase of this passage see "Two World Leaders" in my book *Bible Wonderings*.

[45] Fox, *Original Blessing*, p. 189.

EASTER 5

Torah	Luke 10:25–37
Writing	Galatians 5:1–6
Prophet	Acts 11:1–18
Gospel	Luke 24:13–35

The resurrection story this week comes from Luke's gospel, and the setting returns to Easter Day. Unlike John's story, wherein Jesus continually appears to familiar people, here Jesus appears unrecognized to persons we do not know. This creates a double breakthrough, for we can perhaps more readily place ourselves in the story.

John Dominic Crossan suggests that the Emmaus story can be seen as a parable for the early church's understanding of the presence of the risen Christ. To emphasize the point, Crossan states, "Emmaus never happened. Emmaus always happens."[46] Whether we accept the historicity of this story is secondary to recognizing in it the power of it as *story*, as resurrection appearance, and see in it parallels to our own encounter of the risen Christ, which is hopefully more than a mere historical event also.

The other passages for this week provide elements of shock that ought to be highlighted – our familiarity with the stories can numb us somewhat to the surprises they must have carried to those who lived them, or first heard them. Jesus tells a story where the hero is a Samaritan, of all people. Peter has his world-view challenged to its very core. Finally, Paul addresses bluntly the truth about grace as opposed to those who would rather cling to the law. Breakthrough does not always come easily to us; old *vias* die hard.

---

[46] John Dominic Crossan, *Jesus: a Revolutionary Biography*, (San Francisco: Harper, 1994), p. 197.

EASTER 6

Torah	Matthew 25:31–46
Writing	James 2:1–13
Prophet	Esther 1:1–12
Gospel	John 21:1–14 (15–19)

We return to John for the Gospel, and the appearance of Jesus on the beach, cooking breakfast and providing fishing tips. One can stop the reading at verse 14, and focus on the miraculous catch of fish, symbolically including all the nations of the earth, and make parallels with Matthew 25 and the story of the sheep and the goats. Alternatively one can continue through verse 19 and the conversation about feeding Jesus' sheep. In either case, however, I have stopped the reading prior to the verses where Jesus speaks about Peter's death, seeing these as a distraction from the key stories.

The James text works well with Matthew and the second story from John, as well as complementing the story of Queen Vashti, whose silent defiance serves as the prophetic voice for this week.

Vashti's story is not well-known, and does not appear in other lectionaries (other than the annual reading of the entire book of Esther at the Jewish festival of Purim). Ancient rabbinic sources vary in their views of this brave woman. In some sources, she is seriously maligned. "She was so cruel," reads one commentary, "that she even forced Jewish maidens to spin and weave on the Sabbath."[47]

However, other sources are far more understanding, seeing Ahasuerus as an abusive tyrant, and suggesting that Vashti was within her rights to assert her dignity. Many traditions hold that Ahasuerus had demanded Vashti appear before him naked, or wearing only her crown. With prophetic dignity she refused to suffer such humiliation.[48]

---

[47] Rabbinic source cited in Lois Miriam Wilson, *Miriam, Mary, and Me – Women in the Bible: Stories Retold for Children and Adults*, (Kelowna, BC: Northstone, 1992), p. 19.
[48] *Esther Rabbah 3.13–14*, in Michael E. Williams, ed., *The Storyteller's Companion to the Bible, Vol. Four – Old Testament Women*, (Nashville: Abingdon, 1993), p. 156.

In any event, the power of the story lies in the example of Vashti to hold her ground, and to risk everything to proclaim her self-worth and maintain her self-respect. The fact that this scared the men of the kingdom to panic and fear losing their elevated status that she left her mark.

EASTER 7

Torah	Matthew 20:1–16
Writing	1 Corinthians 1:23–25
Prophet	Esther 4:1, 4–17, 7:1–6, 9–10
Gospel	Matthew 28:16–20

The prophetic witness of Queen Vashti last week is followed by her successor Queen Esther this week. It is tempting to include the entire story, but I recognize that this is simply too lengthy, so I have sought to include enough to set the stage and showcase Esther's prophetic actions on behalf of the Jewish people.

This is accompanied by two stories from Matthew – the parable of the vineyard workers all receiving fair and equal wages, and the story of Jesus' final commission to the disciples, an appropriate text to read at the closing of the Easter season.

The Writing comes from 1 Corinthians, a potent three verses wherein Paul points out that the great oxymoron of a crucified Messiah blasts out of the water the conventional wisdom of the world. "For Paul," writes Marcus Borg, "'Christ crucified' is an indictment of the imperial system of domination that executed Jesus."[49] This, in turn, is the wisdom of God.

---

[49] Marcus Borg, *Reading the Bible Again for the First Time,* (San Francisco: Harper, 2002), p. 256.

PENTECOST SUNDAY

Torah	Numbers 11:24–30
Writing	Proverbs 1:20–33
Prophet	Colossians 3:9b–17
Gospel	Acts 2:1–21

This day is key, serving to close the Easter season while at the same time setting the tone for the upcoming season of Transformation as well.

The Gospel choice is a given – the Acts passage that tells the story of the day of Pentecost and the arrival (although *not* the first appearance, as some will so very mistakenly claim) of God's spirit in the form of fire and wind – primal energy. The dynamic, boundary–breaking work of the spirit is celebrated with prophetic abandon.

Theme 22 in *Original Blessing* wherein Fox speaks about the spirit coming upon all persons and making them prophets inspires the other readings. Accordingly, the Torah reading comes from the Revised Common Lectionary, alternate first reading for Year A. Elitism and status quo are challenged by the outpouring of the spirit on "outsiders" and this theme is further explored in the Writings text from Proverbs, with Wisdom calling out and almost daring us to welcome her into our minds, our hearts, and our lives. For a prophetic text, Colossians 3:9b–17 rounds things out with a presentation of some of the new behaviors to be expected of one who is in Christ.

Thus draws to its conclusion the *via creativa*. We have rebirthed, and we have been reborn. So what? Where do we go from here? There is too much desire and emphasis in "modern, Western" or "post-modern" society to stop here. It feels good. It sells. It has the proverbial "warm fuzzies." But it is incomplete. We must move on, into the realm of compassion. We need to be transformed and transforming.

So we enter the *via transformativa*.

Chapter 8 – *Via Transformativa:*
The Season after Pentecost – living with the cosmic Christ in Ordinary Time

What do we call this season, and these days? In most traditions they are a down time, a simple time, often called the Sundays after Pentecost, or after Trinity. Other traditions name them the Sundays in Ordinary Time (originally meaning that they were counted with ordinal numbers) or Propers (because they were Sundays in their own, proper, right, not "belonging" to a festival season).

In this lectionary, however, they are more than just everyday days, as they form one of the four paths. Thus, because they fall in the *via transformativa*, I have named them Transformativa 1, Transformativa 2, and so forth.

THE FEAST OF THE NAMES OF GOD[50]

(First Sunday after Pentecost/Transformativa 1)

Torah	Exodus 3:5–6, 13–15
Writings	Colossians 1:15–20
Prophet	Isaiah 66:10–13
Gospel	Matthew 16:13–16

In the choice of these scriptures, limiting by and of themselves, a number of images of God come into play. Exodus presents a rather anthropomorphic picture of a God who cares deeply about people and justice, a God who liberates, and who will not be confined by a name or a label – a God at once living and dynamic with a name that is a verb.

The Writings text comes from Colossians (even though last week this same book provided the Prophet reading) in an ancient hymn of praise to the Christ of the cosmos. A vast number of images of Christ are presented here, providing ample room for a preacher to expound upon, and to be in dialogue with, the definitions that come up in the Gospel reading, the somewhat classic text in which Jesus asks the disciples for their take on his identity.

In the brief prophetic text we again see God's compassion, only this time there is the blatant expression of God as mother – an image so sorely in need of proclamation in a culture so saturated with masculine images of the divine.

---

[50] Traditionally this lengthy season has begun with Trinity Sunday. However, giving such prominence to the Trinity with its rather finite limitations on God's identity seems hardly in keeping with Creation Spirituality. Where, for example, does one place Wisdom, or the cosmic Christ?

This is not to denigrate the importance of the Trinity as a vehicle for understanding and expressing God, nor to imply that Creation Spirituality does this. There is without question a place for the Trinity in our *theology*. But I believe that to give it a feast day within the Christian year – to afford it 1/52 of the Christian calendar – can be problematic. At a glance it suggests to too many people that the traditional formula of "Father, Son, and Holy Spirit" is, if not the only, certainly the paramount way to image and express the Divine within Christianity. To counter this, then, I would propose a replacement in title, and texts.

A self-criticism I would note at this point is that all of the images present here are, for all intents and purposes, human. I'll grant that it may be hard to define a burning bush as human, yet we are dealing here with what can really only be defined as a human voice, or at least what Moses experiences as a human voice.

All this is of course extremely limiting as the Bible presents a plethora of images of God that come from the non–human realm of creation as well, but this particular set of images seemed to offer their own balance.

TRANSFORMATIVA 2

Torah	Genesis 38:11–26
Writings	Psalm 46
Prophet	Isaiah 1:10–17
Gospel	Acts 9:36–43

Next week begins the saga of Joseph and his family and, in order to give it some continuity, a portion of the story – which reads as a bit of an intrusion anyway – is given here.

In this week's reading from Genesis Tamar turns the tables (positively) on Judah who has first turned them negatively on her. Isaiah challenges the people to do the justice that God has asked of them in the first place. Indeed, in what might have been perceived as a complete turnaround, Isaiah declares that God is sick and tired of their worship and sacrifices.

Peter and Dorcas (working with the Holy Spirit) turn the tables on death. And the psalmist reminds us that even when nations surround us and scream war, the presence of God and the river of life in our midst are more powerful. God's presence is life. This is stronger than the forces of death, violence, deceit, and evil.

In all of this, people are taking the initiative – one might say the divine initiative – to turn the tables on the world, a fitting way to ease ourselves fully into the *via transformativa*.

TRANSFORMATIVA 3

Torah	Genesis 37:1–11
Writings	Ecclesiastes 3:1–8
Prophet	Revelation 7:1–4, 9–10 (11–17)
Gospel	Acts 2:42–47

Beginning with this Sunday, a couple of semi-continuous streams emerge. The saga of the children of Jacob will be the Torah reading for six weeks, and the Gospel will be taken from the book of Acts. In the case of the former, this is a profound story of transformation that deserves our attention. In the case of the latter, it seems appropriate to read of the transformation in the lives of early Christians following Pentecost.[51]

The story from Genesis this week simply sets the stage for the remainder of the story, presenting some of the family dynamic between Joseph and his father, and Joseph and his brothers.

From Acts, we read of the early Christians living their lives very differently as a new community: the body of Christ. The Writing is the Ecclesiastes poem regarding time, and the Prophet comes from the book of Revelation, reading about the inclusion of an infinite number of people (represented by the number 144,000) from every nation and tribe and language of the earth. While this number has often been seen over the ages as a finite limit it is in fact a symbolic representation of infinity, implying the whole world.

This reading parallels somewhat the Acts passage, broadening the image of who is included in the church. It also may help to "redeem" the book of Revelation, too long abandoned to those who would abuse it and twist it to their purposes, when it has much to offer. Passages such as this one, which speak of inclusion of all manner of persons, have too long been used to exclude. Thus the *via transformativa* can be used here to transform our perception of a long–maligned scripture passage.

---

[51] Not to question the wisdom of the other lectionary compilers too unduly, but the chronology was always a bit confusing for children when we dealt with stories of the early church throughout the Easter season, and then often referred to the last day of that season – Pentecost – as the "birthday of the church."

TRANSFORMATIVA 4

Torah   Genesis 37:12–20, (21–24), 25–27, (28a), 28b–36

Writings   Psalm 57

Prophet   Isaiah 5:1–7

Gospel   Acts 16:16–34

The choppiness of the Genesis passage is for the benefit of those who may wish to follow one track of the story a little more smoothly. It seems quite clear that an ancient biblical editor has blended two accounts into one in this narrative, and some confusion can arise; deleting the verses in parentheses can reduce the confusion.

In this story, we set up the drama within the Jacob family. One brother (Joseph) is favored by the father. The jealous brothers (the details get a bit sketchy depending on whether you read all of the verses or not) seek to get rid of him and lie to their father about it. While in some ways it is little more than prologue, it is the prologue to the story of our lives: everyday family drama, jealousy, mistrust, love, confusion, mixed emotions, misplaced loyalties, and more besides. Against this tableau lies always the opportunity for transformation and for the presence of God to work wonders.

Psalm 57, in the style of many laments, moves in some ways through the four paths. While the images of the *via positiva* are not named, they are present by default. Without an awareness of the goodness of God, and some sense of worthiness, the psalmist would neither bother nor dare to address the divine. The lament portion itself speaks of the *via negativa*, but the words of praise (beginning at verse 5) indicate the breakthrough of the *via creativa*, and move into the *via transformativa* that is celebrated in the last verses. This fits well with many aspects of the Joseph story.

The story of Paul and Silas seems a natural counterpart to this part of Joseph's journey. Likewise, the parable of the vineyard from the Prophet Isaiah reminds us both of God's disappointment in our disobedience, and of God's merciful nature to give second chances.

TRANSFORMATIVA 5

Torah   Genesis 39:1–20 (40:6–23)

Writings   Psalm 1

Prophet   Jeremiah 1:4–10

Gospel   John 15:9-17

The Genesis readings are quite lengthy – even choosing just the piece from chapter 39 is hefty enough. However, it is important to include as much of the story of Joseph and his family as possible, and these two pieces go well together.

The basic part of the reading tells us what happened to Joseph upon his arrival in Egypt, including the story of the attempt by Potiphar's (unnamed) wife to seduce him. In this story we see the integrity of Joseph. If one adds on the portion from chapter 40, we have a chance to see Joseph's gifts of divination shown in jail to two of his fellow prisoners. Again, Joseph's integrity comes to light as he does not hesitate to give good news or bad news when appropriate. In both of these images of Joseph we are reminded of the revolutionary character of honesty. Desired by the world, certainly, yet seldom accepted.

Psalm 1 upholds the desire for integrity, applauding those who delight in God's law and, by extension, condemning those who do not.

The prophetic piece is fairly short and tells of the call of Jeremiah to be a prophet. Like David, he is called as a youth. What is intriguing about Jeremiah's call is that he hesitates, using the excuse of being too young to try and wiggle out of the call. However, God wants no part of it, and tells Jeremiah what to do. Those familiar with the remainder of the book know that he goes on to proclaim God's word in profound and amazing ways.

In the gospel Jesus speaks to the disciples about the importance of loving one another. In so doing, he emphasizes that they are in fact his friends, and that the love of friends truly knows no bounds.

The values in all of these readings present some of the intricacies of trying to follow the *via transformativa.*

TRANSFORMATIVA 6

Torah	Genesis 41:17–40
Writings	2 Corinthians 4:6–10
Prophet	Isaiah 12:1–6
Gospel	Acts 16:9–15

Paul goes to Philippi and, as is his custom, seeks out a Jewish synagogue on the Sabbath, finding an informal gathering at the river. Notice that he is unfazed that it is led by a woman, Lydia, nor does he seem to have a problem staying in her home or discussing theology with her. He later returns to her home after his release from prison (16:40) and encourages the church that has begun to meet in her home and which she presumably leads. This is clearly a vital text regarding the role of women in the early church.

The Prophet text reads more like the Writing, a celebration of God's goodness, a hymn of praise and hope. The Writing text also picks up the sense of hope, celebrating that even in the midst of suffering, one can find reason to celebrate. We live with the cross, and we live with the empty tomb – *via positiva* and *via negativa* are come together in Christ.

Continuing with the saga of Joseph, we read of Pharaoh's dreams and the dilemma in which he finds himself. Joseph interprets the dreams for the Pharaoh (frankly, not a huge task) and Pharaoh in turn names Joseph his prime minister. The story may seem a bit stretched at first glance, but it contains powerful imagery of one's life situation turning over for the good (Joseph) and for one in power (Pharaoh) to call on a very unlikely source for assistance.

TRANSFORMATIVA 7

Torah	Genesis 43:1–5, 15, 44:1–4, 14–18, 24–34,
	or Genesis 43:1–44:34
Writings	Psalm 34
Prophet	Daniel 7:1–14
Gospel	Acts 10:34–43

This day we read of the transformation of Joseph's brothers. Like some of the other sagas in the Bible, the best way to have dealt with the story of Joseph would have been in its entirety, but that would of course be impractical in worship. Even the suggestion of reading two full chapters borders on the ridiculous (although I'll concede that chopping up little bits of two chapters this week is hardly less so). The gist of the story being presented here is that the brothers, presumably based on years of reflection, have changed to more honest beings than in their younger days, and that presents a parable for us.

Peter's speech in response to his conversion experience of the vision of animals on the rooftop makes an intriguing parallel. This is a key text for the *via transformativa* in expressing the understanding of God's universal love and acceptance of all people without showing partiality. May we, like Peter, be so transformed, and similarly taste and see the goodness of our God, as the psalm invites us to do. Peter, like the psalmist, has been rescued from foes, in this case racism and exclusivism.

The apocalyptic vision of Daniel has links to the cosmic Christ, within the phrase "Son of Man." Here a human one – perhaps a prototype of the nation of Israel or, by extension, of the cosmic Christ and then the Body of Christ – comes with greater power than huge and terrifying beasts, representing the powers of this world.

It is no mere coincidence that the title "Son of Man" or "Human One" is Jesus' preferred way of referring to himself according to the gospels, he being the one who has the power and glory of God. Let us immediately remember that this is within God's definition of power and glory, one that comes not to be served but to serve. Worldviews are transformed yet again.

TRANSFORMATIVA 8

Torah	Genesis 45:1–15
Writings	Romans 8:31–39
Prophet	Isaiah 52:13–53:12
Gospel	Acts 8:26–40

In the crowning moment of the family saga, Joseph and his brothers reconcile. Forgiveness happens. Transformation happens. New life happens.

In Paul's letter to the Romans, we read that nothing – repeat, nothing – can separate us from God's love in Christ Jesus. The list that Paul gives simply serves to drive the point home, and this sets us up for the amazing story in Acts, where one who is excluded and hungering for acceptance finds it as Philip expounds on one of the servant songs from Isaiah (which is the Prophet reading for today). Philip's act of baptizing the man and thus bringing him fully into the Christian community is a bold statement of the transforming ministry of the church, lost over the ages. This is a prime example of "What Would Jesus Do?" The answer is clear: accept the unaccepted, widen the circle, and set another place at the table.

Too often the church acts as if the issue is "what might Jesus think about that" when the issue is "what would Jesus do?" This is what appears to have happened with the addition of verse 37, wherein someone added a theological confessional statement to what they presumably felt was an overly simplistic baptismal ritual. Philip encountered someone in need, and responded to that need, offering new life in Christ. Later the church came along and said, "that's not enough. We need to have a creedal statement and theological discussion first," even if it did amount to just one verse. A professor of mine once stated, "Jesus came proclaiming the way to the kingdom of God. The church came along and set up a tollbooth. What a letdown."

TRANSFORMATIVA 9

Torah	Exodus 1:(1–5) 6–22
Writings	Psalm 124
Prophet	Isaiah 44:21–27
Gospel	Mark 10:46–52

This week begins a series of seven readings from Exodus, starting with the story of the oppression of the Hebrew people, the command to kill the male babies, and the brave actions of the midwives Shipraph and Puah. The reading stops short of the birth of Moses, so as to allow us to focus on the earlier action without distraction.

For the biblical author to name the women is a powerful act. Furthermore, to read that they – slaves and midwives – are summoned into the presence of the Pharaoh, the most powerful man in the Mediterranean world at the time (and who is himself never named in the narrative) is astonishing. Shiphrah and Puah are clearly the focus of this story. Their actions speak to us, and we need to listen.

Similarly, Bartimaeus dares to speak out, even when those around him would try to silence him. Because of his faith and a willingness to speak out and claim what is rightfully his, Bartimaeus gets Jesus' attention, and is thus able to receive healing. Do we dare to claim the healing, the new life that we deserve? This text can speak to oppressed peoples everywhere.

Both Psalm 124 and Isaiah 44 celebrate God's forgiveness and presence, complementing the other readings.

TRANSFORMATIVA 10

Torah	Exodus 2:1–10
Writings	Psalm 121
Prophet	Isaiah 6:1–8
Gospel	Luke 5:1–11

This week we read of the birth of Moses and the intervention of Jochebed, Miriam, and the unnamed Egyptian princess in ensuring his survival. The princess would undoubtedly be aware of her father's edict and yet she has no apparent problem in breaking the law. In the crowning irony of the story, Moses' mother Jochebed is paid to nurse her own child.

Psalm 121 and the assurance of God's presence sung by pilgrims on their way to Jerusalem echo the presence of God as protector in this story.

The other two readings are about call – Isaiah being challenged, forgiven, and sent while he is going about his business in the Temple, and Jesus calling Simon, James, and John to be disciples. In both of these stories, persons who are called come to an awareness of their sinfulness, and feel unworthy of the call to service. Yet in both cases, this is not an impediment to discipleship.

TRANSFORMATIVA 11

Torah	Exodus 3:1–12a
Writings	Hebrews 4:1–13
Prophet	Jeremiah 20:(1–6) 7–18
Gospel	Luke 1:26–38

As last week we read the calling of a prophet and some disciples, so this week we read the call to Moses. The rabbis provided an intriguing story that indicates reasons for God's choice of Moses:

> When Moses was in Midian keeping sheep for his father-in-law, Jethro, one of his young sheep ran away. Moses left the rest of the flock to run after the lamb that fled. The faster Moses ran and the more he shouted, the faster the sheep ran ahead of him. Finally, the sheep found a quiet pool in a shady spot and stopped to drink. When Moses saw this, he said, "How foolish I was. You only wanted a drink, and by chasing after you I made the situation even worse. You must be tired by now." So he placed the lamb on his shoulder and carried it back to the flock. Seeing Moses' compassion for the sheep, God said, "This is the one I want to lead my people out of slavery in Egypt."[52]

This story suggests that the choice of Moses was not predetermined but, more importantly, based on compassion, which is highly logical and surely in keeping with the *via transformativa*. It's an intriguing piece for contemplation.

The second call story is of the prophet Mary of Nazareth. Usually read during Advent, and thus somewhat lost in the context of her role as mother of Jesus, I place the story here to ground it more firmly as a call story. An intriguing aspect of this story is that there is far less reluctance to accept the call to ministry on Mary's part than there is on the part of most men who are called (compare Moses, Isaiah, Jeremiah for example). Mary simply expresses surprise before agreeing.

---

[52] *Exodus Rabbah 2.2*, cited in Michael Williams, ed., *Storyteller's Companion to the Bible, Vol. 2, Exodus–Joshua*, (Nashville: Abingdon, 1992), p. 40.

Hebrews speaks of entering God's rest (something a prophet must surely long for!) and Jeremiah utters the honest cry of a prophet who has reached the point of burnout. There is exasperation, and there is praise, and there is a plea for justice, and there is anger, and there is frustration. Above all there is honesty.

Being a disciple, being a prophet (remember, we are all called to be prophets – this is part of the *via transformativa*) is not always easy, not always enjoyable, not always rewarding. Denying our feelings is hardly healthy. God allows for, and requires, honest expression of our feelings.

Psalm 137 (see Lent 5, above pp. XX) is a prime example of expressing honest – and harsh feelings – in scripture. Likewise, on the cross, quoting Psalm 22, Jesus expresses a sense of abandonment. Episcopal priest M.R. Ritley speaks of the harm done by telling children that their feelings are wrong. "The process of attenuating and crippling people begins in childhood, begins with the denial of our feelings. 'Oh, you do not want to throw your baby sister in the garbage!' Well, you probably did at that moment. 'Now, aren't you sorry you hit Cousin Bobby?' No, not even remotely."[53]

Jeremiah gives us permission to be perfectly honest with God. God can take it. After all God is, well, God.

---

[53] L. William Countryman and M.R. Ritley, *Gifted by Otherness: Gay and Lesbian Christians in the Church*, (Harrisburg, PA: Morehouse, 2001), p. 70.

Transformativa 12

Torah	Exodus 13:17–22 (14:10–31)
Writings	Psalm 12
Prophet	Matthew 21:23–32
Gospel	Luke 13:10–17

The story of the events surrounding the departure from Egypt is extremely lengthy, and extremely difficult to read. I do not wish necessarily to overly-edit and sanitize and so I provide the option of reading the part of the story that includes the death of the Egyptian solders. However, my preference would be the small lection from Exodus 13 so as to focus on the presence of God in the process, rather than on the portions with which we are more familiar, often as interpreted by Hollywood. If using the optional verses as well, the following rabbinic tale provides helpful insight:

> The story goes that the angels were celebrating when the Israelites crossed the sea and were freed. God told them to stop celebrating and explained to the angels that while some of God's creatures had just reached freedom, some of God's creatures had just been destroyed. It was not a reason to celebrate. Maybe one day we will learn to tell stories that both celebrate and allow us to be compassionate toward those who hurt. Compassion, like forgiveness, is part of God's way.[54]

This week's Prophet comes from one of the gospels, and both it and the Gospel text contain challenges by Jesus to the religious leadership.

In the Matthew text, in a conversation over authority, the leaders are stymied in a simple rabbinic argument, and Jesus tells them that, while they are dithering over theology, the ones whom they think are on the outside will in fact enter into the realm of God. In a similar vein, in Luke's Gospel Jesus transforms people's understanding of how to sanctify the Sabbath, as he restores healing/fullness of life to a woman who has been bent over for a

---

[54] Rabbi Adam Morris, in *Seasons of the Spirit: Congregational Life – Pentecost 2, 2005*, (Kelowna, BC: Wood Lake Books, 2005), p. 30.

generation. The nature of the "spirit" (verse 11, NRSV) that has disabled her is not clear; we are left to wonder whether it is a physical ailment or social ostracization. But Jesus enables her to stand tall, to claim her personhood. How do we keep the Sabbath day holy? By restoring life and wholeness and freedom and justice to those who have had it denied them for too long.

TRANSFORMATIVA 13

Torah	Exodus 16:1–15, 17:1–7
Writings	1 Corinthians 11:23–28
Prophet	Isaiah 42:14–17
Gospel	Mark 12:13–17

"You will do things on my terms," God seems to be saying in both Isaiah and Exodus. When the people ask for food, God provides it, but just enough for their daily needs, no more. Extra can be kept over the Sabbath, but not any other days.

From 1 Corinthians comes the simple instruction for keeping the Eucharist. Again, in its context, Paul has provided this as an antidote to the wasteful extravagance of the Corinthian church.

In the gospel, when challenged by religious leaders with what they thought was a simple question regarding taxes, Jesus turns it into both a profound political statement and cosmic joke. Give the emperor what is due the emperor, and give God what is due God.

Which is everything.

TRANSFORMATIVA 14

Torah	Exodus 20:1–17 (*or* Deuteronomy 5:6 – 21)[55]
Writings	Galatians 5:13–25
Prophet	Luke 3:1–14
Gospel	Matthew 12:1–8

This week's readings all contain instruction on how to live in God's way, as opposed to our own. Consequently they are all passages that can easily get misused.

The ten commandments (or ten "words" in Hebrew) are guides for the ancient Hebrew community as they seek to establish themselves as a nation in the wilderness. A curious difference between the versions in Exodus and Deuteronomy is found in the statement regarding observing the Sabbath. Exodus states that we are to observe it because God created the universe in six days, and rested on the seventh. Deuteronomy however tells the people to keep a Sabbath day as a memorial to the fact that they were once slaves in Egypt, and God brought them out. The distinction clearly flavors the passage, and you are invited to choose either one.[56]

The primacy given to them in the tradition – even to the point of lawsuits in the United States as to whether or not they ought to be displayed in civil courtrooms as being foundational of our entire society – seems more than a little overdone. Thus, the Gospel for this day is a story in which Jesus himself challenges the act of taking them too literally.

This week's Prophet is John the Baptizer (usually encountered in Advent and the Season after the Epiphany) calling us to new and transformative ways of living.

The text from Galatians invites us to move beyond the Law (as Paul calls it), into freedom in Christ. Paul takes great pains throughout Galatians and other writings to tackle the false notion that freedom in Christ means doing whatever we please. Rather Christ has liberated us from the system of earning and losing points

---

[55] For a paraphrase of this story see "Torah Talk" in my book *Bible Wonderings*.

[56] One could actually read both passages, and then comment on the difference between the two.

106

that the Law seems to impose on us, and the sense of doom and failure implicit therein. Christ sets us free to a whole new way of living.

The contrast between "flesh" and "spirit" in Galatians, according to Marcus Borg, is akin to Paul's other references to life "in Adam" as opposed to life "in Christ."

> "Flesh" here does not mean our physical bodies, as if there were something wrong with physical existence or enjoying our bodies. Rather, "life according to the flesh" and "life according to the Spirit" refer to "life in Adam" and "life in Christ" as two ways of living our embodied existence...
>
> The metaphor of dying to an old way of being is also central to Paul's ethic of transformation. We are to become "sacrifices," an obvious image for death. The result is to be no longer conformed to this age, but to be transformed.[57]

Eugene Peterson's paraphrase of this passage provides a powerful and fresh understanding to what are sometimes seen as a laundry list of vices. As a contrast to loving others as ourselves, Peterson translates verse 17 to read "there is a root of sinful self-interest in us that is at odds with a free spirit," and then renders verses 19–23:

> It is obvious what kind of life develops out of trying to get your own way all the time: repetitive, loveless, cheap sex; a stinking accumulation of mental and emotional garbage; frenzied and joyless grabs for happiness; trinket gods; magic-show religion; paranoid loneliness; cutthroat competition; all-consuming-yet-never-satisfied wants; a brutal temper; an impotence to love or be loved; divided homes and divided lives; small-minded and lopsided pursuits; the vicious habit of depersonalizing everyone into a rival; uncontrolled and uncontrollable addictions; ugly parodies of community. I could go on...
>
> But what happens when we live God's way? He brings gifts into our lives, much the same way that fruit appears in an orchard – things like affection for others,

---

57 Borg, *Reading the Bible Again*, pp. 248–249.

exuberance about life, serenity. We develop a willingness to stick with things, a sense of compassion in the heart, and a conviction that a basic holiness permeates things and people. We find ourselves involved in loyal commitments, not needing to force our way in life, able to marshal and direct our energies wisely.[58]

A pretty good description of the *via transformativa,* I should think.

---

[58] Eugene H. Peterson, *The MESSAGE: The Bible in Contemporary Language* (Colorado Springs: NavPress, 2002).

TRANSFORMATIVA 15

Torah	Exodus 23:1–9
Writings	Galatians 3:23–28
Prophet	Luke 1:46–55
Gospel	John 8:1–11

This week provides for a rather unusual combination of readings. Firstly, Exodus 23:1–9, a text that does not appear in other lectionaries but is a portion of additional laws of ancient Israel, displaying the compassion of God – and the nation. Of particular note are concerns for the poor, the alien, and even one's enemy (verses 4–5).

The Galatians text is more familiar, and complements the Exodus reading with its language of inclusion in the Christian community. Yes, we are literally different, but in the Body of Christ these differences and distinctions do not matter.

The Gospel story is worth including as story, I think, even though the vast majority of biblical scholars consider it apocryphal. It is a profound story about judging others and, considering the work of the Jesus Seminar in questioning many of the teachings of Jesus, I decided that there was probably as much reason to include this passage as several others.

The use of the Magnificat is one of only two times in this lectionary that a text is repeated (it was read also on Advent 4; portions of Exodus 3 were read on Transformativa 11 as well as the Feast of the Names of God). This is for two reasons: firstly, it is a powerful text that bears repeating, and secondly, it seems necessary to include it in the Advent cycle, and also to give it a hearing outside of that cycle so it can receive a different focus.

Outside of the season of Advent, where it tends to get muffled in the excitement of the coming of Christ, this text is more likely to command our attention and invite our participation.

Transformativa 16

Torah	Genesis 32:22–31
Writings	Psalm 13
Prophet	Isaiah 64:1–8
Gospel	John 3:1–17[59]

We now leave the Exodus story, and will read twice more from Genesis and once from the book of Numbers before moving elsewhere for Torah readings for the remainder of the lectionary.

Jacob and Nicodemus struggle at night with questions. Who is God? Where is God? Both seem caught in borderlands, shadowlands, between what they know and what they do not know. Do they dare go forward? Do we? This is part of the *via transformativa* too, for like every other part of the journey there are still questions. How will we be changed?

Accordingly, both of these texts could fit very nicely in the *via negativa*, and I had contemplated placing them there, but in the context of the *via transformativa* they push us a little further, I think, to focus on the changes that take place within the characters. It is the ending of the story that matters, and the "next chapter" that matters; not necessarily in the literal sense, however. What Jacob and Nicodemus do next is not nearly as important as what we might do after we struggle with God and our demons in the night, or when we are challenged to contemplate the movement of the spirit and allow ourselves to be born from above, over and over and over again.

Powerful pleas come through in the other readings: a classic psalm of lament, and Isaiah's cry to God to tear open the heavens and come down. Again, this latter text could fit well in many other seasons. The Revised Common and Roman lectionaries place it in Advent, because of its sense of longing and looking forward to God's arrival. I had contemplated placing it on Easter Sunday, as a sort of prelude to reading the resurrection gospel – "Oh that you would tear open the heavens (tomb) and come down (break through)."

---

[59] For a paraphrase of this story see "Born Again?" in my book *Bible Wonderings*.

Placing it here, we might read it as the words of Jacob crying out in the night, or the wonderings of Nicodemus, longing for the breakthrough that he encounters in Jesus, and thus walks away transformed.

TRANSFORMATIVA 17

Torah	Genesis 33:1–20
Writings	Ephesians 2:11–22
Prophet	1 Samuel 2:1–10
Gospel	Luke 19:1–10[60]

Those who are far off are brought together – Jews and Gentiles (in the case of Ephesians) and Jacob and Esau (in the case of Genesis). Perceptions are challenged: the brother who had been so feared is not the threat that Jacob had thought him to be. Hostility between Jew and Gentile, symbolized by the Law that had separated them, is gone because Christ has rendered the Law moot.

The Prophet that speaks to us this week is Hannah, with words that are later echoed by Mary. The justice and reconciliation spoken by her complement the first two readings, and speak to the Gospel, the story of Zacchaeus.

Much transformation takes place in this story. Some have seen in it the reclamation of a sinful tax collector, but that is in fact probably not the case. Common translations and readings of the text have placed Zacchaeus' words in the future tense suggesting that, because of having been recognized and summoned by Jesus, he will mend his ways and become a wonderful and honest person. But read the text more closely.

The verbs are *not* in the future tense in the original Greek, but in the present tense. A more legitimate translation of the text would have Zacchaeus saying, in essence, "Look, I give half of my possessions to the poor, and if I defraud anyone of anything I pay back four times as much." In other words, "I already do these things. But no one believes me." There is nothing in the text itself to support that Zacchaeus is a cheat, or that he repents. Yet that is how most people have understood it. Perhaps because we would rather deal with a story of a nasty, cheating person being turned into a nice, honest person by Jesus, than with a story about people's perceptions being changed. But, like it or not, that is what the Bible gives us.

---

[60] For a paraphrase of this story see "Crowd Conversion" in my book *Bible Wonderings*.

If Zacchaeus is already dealing justly and compassionately in his day-to-day business, then the ones who are being "converted" in this story are the ones who have perceived him as dishonest and thus labeled him an outcast and undesirable based on who he is. This is a powerful *via transformativa* text for those in the gay, lesbian, bisexual and transgender community who are marginalized on the basis of identity. It also speaks well to those of any number of faiths, races, skin colors, and other groups who may at any time and in any place be placed on social, ecclesiastical, or other "hit lists" because of identity and/or association. Zacchaeus is transformed from one who has been hidden, or must climb a tree in order to see and be seen, to one who is named a child of Abraham and in whose home Jesus will be pleased to dine. The crowd is transformed in their recognition of who their neighbor is. At least we can only hope.

TRANSFORMATIVA 18

Torah	Numbers 27:1–11
Writings	Psalm 133
Prophet	Joel 2:25–29 (30–32)
Gospel	Mark 7:24–30

The story of Mahlah, Noah, Hoglah, Milcah, and Tirzah claiming their inheritance is a very unfamiliar passage of scripture. The five brave women approach Moses and request inheritance rights (albeit to preserve the name of their father Zelophehad) and the rights are granted, by God's decree. The rights are secondary to those of sons, but have primacy over those of the man's brothers. It is a story that deserves telling.

A story of sisters is complemented with a short psalm celebrating brothers getting along, and God pouring out the spirit on all flesh – specifically men and women, young and old, slave and free. One need push the text just a tiny bit to assure that reference to all flesh includes animals. Why wouldn't it? Just because they are not named, presumably they would be included – they do, after all, have flesh.

The passage is again loosed from its traditional Pentecost mooring to give it a little more individuality, and the verses preceding the familiar lection have been added with the closing verses given as an option.

In the Gospel we read another story of a courageous woman, in this case challenging Jesus about who is to inherit the healing power that Jesus dispenses. Yet he repents, he changes, and he allows himself to be transformed. In this – as in other stories such as Gethsemane and on the cross – we see the humanness of Jesus, and can allow it to help us come to terms with, accept, and celebrate our own humanness. As someone at a conference I attended once expressed it, "I like knowing that if Jesus can have a bad hair day, so can I."

TRANSFORMATIVA 19

(Omit if used during the Season after the Epiphany.)

Torah	Matthew 5:1–12 *or* Luke 6:20–26
Writings	Psalm 19
Prophet	Ezekiel 37:1–14
Gospel	John 2:1–12[61]

This week the Torah readings shift from Hebrew scriptures to texts from the gospels, and will continue that pattern through the remainder of the year. A logical place to begin seemed with the beatitudes. At the outset we must readily concede that there are substantial differences between Matthew's beatitudes and Luke's, but I nonetheless offer the two as options. This allows you to choose according to your desired emphasis.

Various translations render the opening word of the beatitudes in a variety of ways, generally either "blessed" or "happy" and, in the case of the second half of the Lucan version, either "woe to you" or "cursed are you." The Jesus Seminar gave a red rating (indicating they are probably Jesus' genuine words) to much of the first part of Luke's text, rendering them "Congratulations, you poor!" etc. They gave a black rating (extremely unlikely to be the words of Jesus) to the second half, which they rendered "Damn you rich!" etc.[62]

Neil Douglas-Klotz has done ground-breaking work seeking to reconstruct the sayings of Jesus in the original Aramaic. He has offered a variety of renderings of Matthew's beatitudes, using such introductory words as "Happy and aligned with the One are those who..." and "Tuned to the Source..." and "Healed are those who..."[63] Such concepts take the text out of the "religious" realm and make it more accessible and, I believe, more transforming.

The other readings all contain elements of complete reversal as well: the heavens declare God's praise to the ends of the earth, yet without sound; dead bones come to life; water becomes wine.

---

[61] For a modern-day paraphrase of this story see "After the Wedding" in my book *Bible Wonderings*.

[62] Robert W. Funk, et al, *The Five Gospels*, p. 289.

[63] Douglas-Klotz, *Prayers of the Cosmos*, p. 47.

Within these texts are sub-themes that challenge some of our preconceptions and sensibilities as well.

Psalm 19 celebrates God's "law" (always a dismal translation of *torah*) and thus challenges those of us who are preconditioned to think of law – or even of the Hebrew scriptures – as rigid legalism to be avoided at all costs. Instead we are invited to remember that *torah* is not law in our twenty-first century, courtroom understanding, but God's liberating way. It can in fact be described as "sweeter than honey."

The story of the wedding at Cana challenges us with the image of a God who sees life as a celebration, and who wants the celebration to continue. We have an image of Jesus being reluctant to leap into ministry. And we have an image of Mary taking the initiative in ministry.

All in all, this week is quite a feast of transformativa.

TRANSFORMATIVA 20

Torah	Matthew 22:35–39
Writings	Psalm 15
Prophet	Micah 6:1–8
Gospel	John 2:13–22

Who may dwell in God's tent? Those who do God's will. What is God's will? Seek justice, love kindness, and walk humbly with God. Yet we have turned God's tent/temple into a den of thieves. If only we would learn to love God, and love our neighbor, and love ourselves. An overly simplistic rendering, to be sure, but that is the story today's lections seek to tell.

Community is key here. We are called to live and love in community: God, others, and self. There are no exceptions, nor is it a hierarchy.

We have to love ourselves, or else we cannot love others. We have to love others, or else we cannot love ourselves. And we have to love God, because God first loved us. When we love in this way, we change the world. Fox writes, "The *Via Transformativa* reminds all people that they are already empowered to be instruments of transformation."[64] How do we do this? We seek justice. We love kindness. We walk humbly with out God.

It is that simple. It is that difficult.

---

[64] Fox, *Original Blessing*, p. 299.

TRANSFORMATIVA 21

Torah	Matthew 5:13–16
Writings	Psalm 122
Prophet	Revelation 3:14–22
Gospel	John 9:1–41

Many people may be familiar with Revelation 3:20 ("Behold, I stand at the door and knock…"), but perhaps not with the letter to the church at Laodicea from which the quotation comes. I struggled with which of the letters to the seven churches to include, and felt that this one – with the concern about the church being neither hot nor cold – seemed a good choice for today's world.[65]

The story of Jesus healing the man born blind speaks to how we see and perceive things, which can open up an intriguing dialogue with the Revelation text. It invites a conversation with Matthew as well. How are we – or are we not – like salt and light?

Psalm 122 is a joyous celebration about being in God's presence. It enters into conversation with the other texts in verse 9 where the psalmist pledges devotion to God.

---

[65] A preacher may want to substitute another of the letters for a particular situation. Either way, it is good to read these letters from time to time; the Revised Common and Roman lectionaries disregard them.

TRANSFORMATIVA 22

(Omit if used during the Season after the Epiphany.)

Torah	Matthew 5:21–24
Writings	Galatians 2:(15–18) 19–21
Prophet	2 Samuel 6:1–5, 12–19
Gospel	Mark 5:25–34

In this portion of the Sermon on the Mount Jesus seeks to expand our understanding of the Law. More than technicalities, it is our intent that matters.

Intent is the key to the woman's actions in the story from Mark as well. Without making any fuss, she seeks to touch Jesus' cloak quietly and discreetly, believing that this can somehow change her situation. Jesus, in turn, is intent on giving her more: naming her ("Daughter") and proclaiming her healed.

The Prophet text tells of David bringing the ark into Jerusalem, with the ensuing celebration that includes dancing, merriment, and the sharing of food. (Following the lead of other lectionaries, I have left out the portion that deals with the death of Uzzah.)

In Galatians, we read more of Paul's explanation of justification by grace. Marcus Borg points out that this text, like much of Paul's writing, does not feed into the "Jesus died for my sins because I was a bad person" explanation, but rather the understanding of Christ's death as showing the way to God, as "the embodiment or incarnation of the path of internal psychological and spiritual transformation that lies at the center of the Christian life."[66]

We celebrate the entry into the new Jerusalem, the new life, and the new realities to which Christ leads us.

---

[66] Borg, *Heart of Christianity*, p. 93.

TRANSFORMATIVA 23

Torah	Matthew 5:33–42
Writings	Romans 5:(1–5) 6–11
Prophet	Luke 3:15–18
Gospel	Matthew 9:9–13

From the Sermon on the Mount we have more teaching about going the extra mile – literally, in this case. From a bit later in the same gospel we read the call of Matthew and follow on to conversation with the Pharisees about eating with sinners. From Romans, more conversation about being saved by grace – an appropriate piece to complement the other two texts. Lastly from Luke, a short piece regarding the prophet John the Baptizer, again a text usually encountered in the Advent-Christmas-Epiphany cycle.

This text has endured some misuse over the centuries, as some see in it an image of judgment over different kinds of people, some of us being wheat and others chaff. However if we remember that wheat and chaff come from the same stalk of wheat the image changes. The image here is seems to be of Christ sifting from us those aspects of our individual lives that need to be shed, that in the process of transformation we might be rid of our chaff (read: baggage) and bear the fruit of the Spirit of new life, to borrow Paul's language.

TRANSFORMATIVA 24

Torah	Luke 6:27–36
Writings	Ruth 1:1–18
Prophet	Romans 12:9–21
Gospel	Mark 7:14–23

For the teaching on loving one's enemies I have turned to Luke's version – with a bit of overlap with last week's Torah reading from Matthew. This same theme gets carried through in the Romans text, and in Ruth.

In the Mark text Jesus speaks of the things that defile us – the things that come from the inside, rather than from outside. In challenging those who were obsessed with purity laws about clean and unclean, Jesus takes the conversation to a deeper level. The real thing that corrupts community is not the stuff that goes through the digestive tract, but what passes through the heart – our thoughts, our words, and our deeds. It is compassion that counts, not purity regulations.

This can be a good week to explore xenophobia, and how rather than fearing what is outside of us we can invite the cosmic Christ to transform us from the inside out. Just as what is inside of us can defile us, so can it be the thing that cleanses us, and transforms us.

TRANSFORMATIVA 25

Torah	Luke 6:37–42
Writings	James 2:14–26
Prophet	2 Kings 5:1–14
Gospel	Mark 2:1–12

The advice Jesus gives on not judging could be applied to Naaman, who almost misses out on being healed because of his preconceptions. Similarly, preconceptions come into play in the other stories this week as well: preconceptions about the relationship between sin and illness, about what it is to forgive sin, about the relationship between faith and works. Do we do good works to gain salvation? No. But we cannot help but do good works *because* of salvation. This is the *via transformativa*. If we have truly experienced God's grace – another word for *via creativa* – then we cannot help but be transformed, we cannot help but want to respond by living lives of compassion, of justice, of service in response.

The language is not the issue – whether we wish to speak of being saved, born again, experiencing new life, touched by grace, *via creativa*, enlightened, or transformed – it is the experience that matters. It is the faith that results in new action (works) that is the *via transformativa*.

TRANSFORMATIVA 26

Torah	Matthew 11:16–19
Writings	Romans 10:5–17
Prophet	James 3:1–12
Gospel	Luke 21:5–19

It may seem immediately strange to have used James as source for the Writing last week, and the Prophet this week, and I will readily admit that this is quite arbitrary. But as I address in Chapter 3, some of the divisions are quite fluid. Indeed, the Matthew text could probably just as well have served as Prophet this week.

Our tongue can get us in trouble (shades of the teaching two weeks ago about how what comes out of us is what defiles us). Jesus is called names. The disciples will be persecuted. We question. We do not understand, and yet...life goes on. Wisdom *(Sophia* in Greek) is vindicated by her deeds.

I have chosen to go with the Matthew version of this text this week (Luke 7:35 says "Wisdom is vindicated by her children") as a stronger identification of Jesus with Wisdom. Jann Aldredge-Clanton, while recognizing that the Lucan version is probably more accurate, suggests that "in Matthew's Gospel, Jesus is not just the last and greatest of Sophia's children, but is Sophia herself in the flesh. In other words, Jesus is not merely Sophia's child nor Sophia's prophet, but Sophia incarnate."[67]

---

[67] Aldredge-Clanton, *In Search of the Christ-Sophia*, p. 23.

TRANSFORMATIVA 27

Torah	Matthew 13:31–33
Writings	Colossians 2:11–15
Prophet	Revelation 21:1–6, 9–14, 22–26
Gospel	Matthew 18:1–4

We clothe ourselves anew, as children, and enter one of the wondrous gates into the glorious presence of God in the new city. Ultimate *via transformativa*, I suppose. We need our dreams. Yet, it must be more than just a dream, as well.

Writing to a persecuted church, the author of Revelation proclaimed the power of God in Christ to overturn the powers of the world and establish a reign of justice, and the truth of that promise becomes real. While many want to see Revelation as a futuristic vision, it is more a book about living in the now. It is a book about recognizing the power of God in the upside-down, seeming weakness of Jesus, which is much greater than the apparent but flimsy powers of the world. This in turn is borne out by today's gospel texts.

I have chosen two parables about the realm of God, the mustard tree and the yeast, which both require a close look. They may be too familiar for us to miss the surprises they bring. Dominic Crossan paints a vivid, and less than romantic, picture of the image of the mustard tree:

> The mustard plant is dangerous even when domesticated in the garden and is deadly when growing wild in the grain fields. And those nesting birds, which might strike us as charming, represented to ancient farmers a permanent danger to the seed and grain. The point, in other words, is not just that the mustard plant starts as a proverbially small seed and grows into a shrub of three, four, or even more feet in height. It is that it tends to take over where it is not wanted, that it tends to get out of control where it is not wanted, and it tends to attract birds within cultivated areas, where they are not particularly desired. And that, said Jesus,

was what the Kingdom was like. Like a pungent shrub with dangerous takeover properties.[68]

Andrew Harvey points out the subversive nature of the parable of the yeast:

> Judaism regarded leaven as a symbol of corruption, while unleavened bread stood for what is holy; Jesus is here reversing all the accepted values of his world. To make the Kingdom of heaven "leaven," which has to be hidden (and by a woman!), implicitly mocks all conventional notions of the "holy" and "unholy" as well as rooting the business of the Kingdom firmly in the most ordinary, even banal activities. The work of the Spirit, Jesus is implying, is everywhere, in all things, and not merely in those things that men (and they usually were men) designated holy and valuable: it is a work that begins by being hidden and mysterious, like the work of leaven in bread, but in the end, as when the bread is leavened and edible, the invisible presence and power of God's grace becomes obvious.[69]

We are invited to become like a child, and enter this wondrous Kingdom – itself transformed and transforming, and a place where we will continue to do the same.

Next week, we begin the cycle all over again. Because the paths are not linear, the journey does not end. We dance in a circle.

---

[68] Crossan, *Jesus: a Revolutionary Biography*, p. 83.

[69] Andrew Harvey, *Son of Man: The Mystical Path to Christ*, (New York: Jeremy P. Tarcher, 1999), p. 20.

ALL SAINTS' DAY

Via positiva	Job 1:1-22 (2:1-10)
Via negativa	Job 23:1-9, 16-17
Via creativa	Job 38:1-18 (19-41)
Via transformativa	Job 42:1-6
Epilogue	Job 42:7-17

All Saints' Day presents a wonderful opportunity to explore what it is to be a saint – that is, a holy one, or one who is set apart for serving God. The story of Job seems an excellent vehicle for doing this.

The lections here closely parallel the readings in the Revised Common Lectionary for four weeks of Year B. On closer examination, one can see that they really are a delightful microcosm of the four paths. Beyond that, they show us aspects of this person called Job, and in so doing invite us to ponder how the four paths intersect with our saintly living.

We begin with the simple story of someone named Job. It is important to recognize at the outset that this is a work of fiction. God does not sit around with the accuser (a being who is closer to our definition of devil's advocate than devil) and offer up the lives of earthly beings just to prove a point. However, in a work of fiction anything goes, and so this device is available to the storyteller for the purposes of making the point here.

Job is good. We do not have the right to question this, because we are dealing with story, and thus have to accept what the storyteller gives us. What is amazing about Job is that even after he experiences some bizarre, extreme, and tragic events in his life, his response is simply to acknowledge the goodness of God. "God gives, and God takes away," Job declares (1:21) and that seems to be just the way it goes. Can we live like this? Can we accept what life presents simply knowing – and trusting – that somehow God is in the midst of it all?

Job moves on to experience the *via negativa*. Visits from his "friends" (with ones like these, who needs enemies?) are not helpful. Job sits in grief and pain, and as time goes on he gets cranky. "I can accept what God wants to throw at me," he seems to say, "but there's a limit. If I could find God I'd say a thing or two, and I wouldn't be kind about it." Job embraces the darkness, and seeks to find a place within it. While he does not like it, he accepts it.

Then God breaks through.

After the various friends have all said their bit – trying to get Job to admit that he just *has* to be wrong, somewhere, somehow – God speaks for a total of four chapters. The speech is quite intriguing. In this moment of breakthrough God answers Job, although not at all in the way Job seems to have wanted. "Have you ever tried to be God?" is the ultimate question here. Job may be having difficulties, but in the grand scheme of the world, maybe his agenda is not quite so vital.

Through all this, we learn in the final analysis that Job is transformed. Having not fully grasped the expanse of the Divine until now he is left breathless, and apologizes to God. His eyes are re-opened to the newness of God in the world.

The "epilogue" simply recounts the conclusion of the prose story: Job gets back all he lost, and more. Beyond this, he gives his daughters equal inheritance rights to their brothers. With a nod to God's power to transform Job seems to grasp a taste of God's compassion in this moment, reminding us that to be a saint is to be open – always – to the humorous, enormous, wondrous presence of God in the very midst of God's own creation.

Afterword – To Be Continued

So the journey ends. Except that it doesn't, really. It can't.

Time is circular with no real beginning or ending. The year is circular as well.

In forming this lectionary I have only scratched the surface of the scriptures. I have chosen passages that I believe support the ancient paths of Creation Spirituality. I did this intentionally, recognizing that one can readily choose other texts to support other paths and other journeys.

Anyone can look at this and immediately name one or even several passages that most definitely ought to have been included. This is certainly true, not only because my work is not perfect but also because this lectionary is setting out to tell a story, and each of us seeks a different story, and needs a different story.

Every time I go through the cycle of the church seasons, every time I go through what I thought were familiar scripture texts, I am amazed at the new insights that emerge. I think that, at least in part, it is because the story that is embedded within is always finding new ways to enter into our story, and change our lives.

And the story continues…

Donald Schmidt
Bellevue, Washington

Appendix 1 – Lectionaries in Jewish and Christian tradition

This chapter appeared near the beginning of the original book. However, for many it seemed superlative, while other found it key and informative. So rather than discard it I have simply moved it.

We worship, no matter who we are. We seek – and I daresay, no matter how cynical we are, we at least in some small measure find – the divine. Upon encountering it we look for ways to give thanks and to offer praise. At other times we may want to experience a deeper mystery. At still other times we may need to question God, perhaps to express anger sometimes, and to be in all manner of dialogue.

As human beings, we tend to default into doing this in some kind of structured way, whether as individuals or as gathered community. When we do, we want to tell our story. One of the key things that connects us to one another – and even that gives us identity as individuals – is indeed our story.

To remember where we have been, what we have done, and what has happened to us is to remember who we are. Re-enacting this story, individually and corporately, reinforces that identity. Without it, we become lost. This is behind the annual telling of story liturgically in settings both sacred and secular. For example, the world celebrates Christmas – whether in a cathedral with incense and scripture and Eucharist or with an annual parade down an avenue in New York City – because it has to. We have to remember; remembering tells us who we are.

Similarly, we crave ritual. Without ritual we become detached from our world – so much so that, when we lose or abandon one ritual, we tend to pick up another almost immediately to take its place.

The way in which we structure our ritual can in turn have a profound effect on how we view, experience, understand, and express the divine. Our ritual is intrinsically connected to the story we seek to tell.

For Christians who gather in corporate worship both the liturgical year and the lectionary help to shape our understanding of God and Christ. This is also true, I believe, for non–lectionary churches, or those that follow a very loosely-structured lectionary, using obvious seasonal choices of scriptures for festival times. Still others create "mini-lectionaries" or sermon series. We tend to follow patterns and seasons of one kind or another, whether of the greater ecumenical community or of a smaller, perhaps denominational community or individual.

Rather than simply serving as a convenient way to provide Bible readings and other liturgical resources, a lectionary – any lectionary – sets a pattern, a format, a sense of predictability, a framework within which we seek to blend the biblical story with *our* story. It is the vehicle through which we tell our faith story each Sunday.

The account of Jesus reading scripture and preaching in the Nazareth synagogue (Luke 4:15–21) indicates the use of a lectionary in early Jewish tradition. Further, the speech of James in Acts 15:21 points to lectionary usage as well, as the apostle speaks of Moses being "read aloud every Sabbath in the synagogues." These two texts suggest that the pattern of reading from the Torah – one of the first five books of the Hebrew scriptures – combined with a *haftorah*, or secondary text intended to illuminate or comment on the first reading, had been firmly established before the time of Christ.

Many scholars believe such a pattern arose during the time of the Babylonian exile (587–535BCE). Without the Temple, synagogue worship became the norm, and a systematic pattern of scripture readings developed to provide continuity and consistency.

By the time of the return from the exile, a three-year lectionary seems to have been established, with the Torah having been divided into 150 portions, accompanied by a reading from the prophets and, in some instances, a reading from the psalms. The practice was known as *lectio continua* due to the fact that the readings followed a simple continuous pattern, and this pattern continued in the earliest days of the Christian church. Both the Roman and Revised Common Lectionaries today use semi-continuous gospel and epistle readings for much of the year, and the Revised Common offers semi-continuous readings from Hebrew scriptures as one of the options in the Season after Pentecost.

The development of the Christian liturgical year, however, soon gave way to lectionary reform, calling for choices of scripture readings that reflected the nuances of seasonal celebrations and emphases. Books of complete scripture readings, known as *lectionaria* (Latin for "readings") came to be circulated. Such books tended to focus on the festival half of the year, that is from Advent to Pentecost.

At the time of the Reformation a number of things happened so far as lectionaries are concerned. Lutherans and Anglicans tended to retain the use of the lectionary with minor changes; Zwingli and Müntzer abolished the use of lectionaries; and Calvin rejected the church year and lectionary but returned the use of *lectio continua*. The response from Rome was swift and long-lasting: Pope Pius V proclaimed in 1570 that the Roman Missal (and the lectionary included therein) would be the norm within the Roman Catholic church throughout the world, and so it would remain for almost 400 years until the reforms of Vatican II in the 1960's.

The Roman Missal included a one-year lectionary with only two lections per Sunday or festival day. Further, in almost all instances these were taken from the gospels and the epistles, with Acts being used only three times and Revelation not at all. The Hebrew scriptures (Old Testament) did not appear on any Sunday, either, but were included at Epiphany, Good Friday, and Easter Vigil. At the time of the second Vatican Council this lectionary formed a starting point for the huge overhaul that was to take place. Some of the readings from the Roman Missal have been retained, although these have been expanded on enormously.

In the meantime other Christian denominations and traditions over the centuries experimented with their own series of Sunday scripture readings that, surprisingly, show a wider variety than one might at first expect.

The Church of England desired to place not only the scriptures but indeed a prayer book in the hands of every worshipper. They promptly adapted the lectionary for their purposes producing a one-year lectionary for use at the weekly Eucharist, again consisting of an epistle and gospel, and over time creating a two-year lectionary for use at services of morning and evening prayer. This latter lectionary became extremely extensive, providing two readings for both morning and evening. It included a wide range of scriptures, seeming to be bound by no constraints other than a desire to expose the worshippers to God's word and to provide for a reading from the Hebrew scriptures and the New Testament at each service.

The ecumenical undertaking that resulted in the Church of South India – a merger of Anglican, Congregational, Methodist, Presbyterian, and Reformed churches in 1947 – produced both a worship book and a lectionary. While this church's liturgical pattern closely resembled that of the Anglicans its lectionary was an entirely new thing altogether. What emerged in their worship book was a one-year lectionary with two sets of readings: four for the first worship service (presumably in the morning) and two for the second (presumably in the evening). The first set is the pattern which has come to be the norm for modern lectionaries: Hebrew scripture, psalm, epistle, gospel. The second set was a more classic "old testament/new testament" pattern.

The Evangelical and Reformed Church in the United States, in its 1947 *Book of Worship*, also provided a "one-year/two-step" lectionary although in this instance the pattern is somewhat reversed from the Church of South India: the first set (printed in full in the worship book, thus for use at the principle service of worship) consists of epistle and gospel; the "Secondary Lectionary" as it is called consists of epistle, gospel, Hebrew scriptures (in that order.) On occasion, the psalms are used simply as readings from the Hebrew scriptures, without any particular liturgical purpose.

One other lectionary of interest prior to Vatican II is from *The Book of Worship* of the Methodist Church in the US. Again we are presented with a one-year lectionary, but this time three readings for each Sunday (Hebrew scripture, epistle – including at various times 12 readings from Acts and one from Revelation – and gospel) along with a psalm or other canticle.

What is intriguing about all of these lectionaries is that, while in many regards they tell a similar story – the life of Jesus, and a fall/redemption theology lived out through the course of the liturgical year – they use quite different scriptures with which to do that. There are, however, some common points that are rather striking:

- Romans 13:(8–10) 11–14 appears on Advent 1 in all of these lectionaries – and in turn lives on in both the Roman and Revised Common lectionaries, in year A.
- Not surprisingly they all tell the story of the resurrection on Easter Sunday – all of them using Mark 16, except for the Church of South India, which preferred John 20:1–18.
- All of the lectionaries tell the story of Jesus appearing to Thomas and the disciples (John 20:19–31) on the 2nd Sunday of Easter.

Many other common points also exist, but the differences far outweigh the commonalities.

The huge and unprecedented reforms of the Second Vatican Council brought about massive changes in the Roman lectionary, which were to have profound effects on the entire Christian world. A *Consilium* on liturgical reform was created in 1964, and one of its 40 subgroups was in turn charged with creating a lectionary. Five key principles guided their work:

1. The scriptures are an essential component of liturgical celebration.
2. Priority is to be given to the Sunday and Feast Day Lectionary.
3. The Lectionary is to contain more scripture.
4. The Lectionary is to be adapted to modern times.
5. The Lectionary is to take into account previous tradition.[70]

The committee drafted a lectionary that went out to 800 scholars, liturgists, and theologians for review, and then was presented to the pope. On April 3, 1969 Pope Paul VI approved the lectionary and declared it to be the mandatory lectionary for the use of the Roman Catholic church beginning with Advent, 1971.

Living up to its mandate, this lectionary has several key features:

---

[70] Normand Bonneau, *The Sunday Lectionary: Ritual Word, Paschal Shape.* (Collegeville, MN: Liturgical Press, 1998), pp. 25–28.

- a 3-year lectionary (each year following, essentially, one of the synoptic gospels – Matthew, Mark, or Luke)
- three readings (plus a psalm) for each Sunday and festival day
- the gospel text is the predominant reading each week
- the first reading is taken from the Hebrew scriptures (except during Easter, when it comes from the Acts of the Apostles)

While it was not surprising that the Roman Catholic church would adopt a new lectionary, or even expand its use of the scriptures, what was more astonishing about this reform was its effect on Protestant denominations, who began to use the Roman lectionary in great numbers. As they began to make adaptations, the Consultation on Common Texts[71] formed a subgroup to amalgamate the various versions of the "Protestant Roman lectionary" and published the *Common Lectionary* in 1983. Feedback from churches led to the *Revised Common Lectionary* in 1992.

Many of the key features of this lectionary are the same as the Roman lectionary, with one key difference. During the Season after Pentecost (or Ordinary Time) two streams of Hebrew scripture texts are included, along with corresponding psalms. One stream, generally preferred by the Evangelical Lutheran Church in America, the Episcopal Church in the United States, and the Church of England, is known as "paired readings" and most closely resembles the Roman lectionary. In this case, the readings have been chosen thematically to complement the gospel texts for the day.

The other stream includes readings that flow in a semi-continuous pattern from Sunday to Sunday, and thus do not necessarily have a thematic link to the gospel text, but rather provide continuity in the Hebrew narrative from which they are derived. Accordingly, scholars on both sides of the liturgical fence

---

[71] A group with representation from major Protestant denominations in the USA and Canada, as well as the Roman Catholic church, the Consultation on Common Texts was charged with finding common wording for significant liturgical texts, such as the Lord's prayer. The CCT was born out of the decision of the Roman Catholic church to begin using the vernacular in worship, another decision of Vatican II.

have drawn up lines for argument in defense of either stream; my hunch is that most people in the pews neither notice nor care.

What is probably of greater concern in terms of the story that the lectionary tells is what goes on in the half of the year devoted to the festival seasons. The Hebrew scriptures are more explicitly used (some would say abused) to predict aspects of the life of Christ, or to attach themselves so explicitly to certain events that they can virtually never be extricated there from. While there is biblical precedent for doing this (read the opening chapters of Matthew's gospel) the liturgical perpetuation of it can do the church and scriptures both a great disservice. This is not to deny people the right to interpret the scriptures this way if they so choose, but to link them constantly through the construct of the church year and lectionary is not helpful.

This is not to condemn any lectionary, but simply to express caution. Few Christians can read Isaiah 9 without thinking of Christmas, or Isaiah 53 without thinking of Good Friday. That is not by and of itself a bad thing – these are powerful texts, and helpful to read and reflect upon in the context of pivotal events in the life of Christ. Yet at the same time we must recognize that their appearance in the lectionary and the church year very intentionally places them within a particular story that the church seeks to tell. It is, however, not the only story that can be told; there are other ways to tell the story of our faith.

A few other lectionaries of note include the one produced by the United Church of Canada in its *Service Book* published in 1969. Undoubtedly influenced by the work being done by the Roman Catholic Church after Vatican II, this was a three-year lectionary with four readings in similar pattern: Hebrew scriptures, psalm, epistle, and gospel. It was a thematic lectionary, even "clustering" readings in thematic groupings, such as treating the passion narrative throughout Lent in Year C. It also included a Season of Creation beginning on the last Sunday of August. The lectionary probably would have seen wider usage were it not for the soaring popularity of the ecumenical Common Lectionary around the same time, and the plethora of resources that came into being to serve it.

In 2000 Australian Lutheran theologian Norman Habel began work on a lectionary for the Season of Creation. This three-year lectionary suggests a short season in September and October each year. The dates include:

- September 1 – Day of Creation (as in Orthodox traditions)
- Four Sundays dealing with different domains of creation
- St Francis of Assisi Day (October 4)
- Blessing of the Animals

Over the course of three years the four central Sundays in the season encompass such themes as Planet Earth, River, Outback, Storm, and Forest, among others. This lectionary is growing in popularity throughout the world, with some slight variance for the northern hemisphere.[72]

Two more worth mentioning are both titled *Uncommon Lectionary*. One by Canadian Tom Bandy tends to have some popularity amongst emerging churches. Rather than providing four readings for the week, based on chapters and verses, this provides only one longer reading designed around "chunks" of scripture. A second reading is provided for the focus of meditation, small groups, and others during the week.[73]

An *Uncommon Lectionary* by John Beverly Butcher – an Episcopal priest in California, and associate of the Jesus Seminar – is suggested to complement or supplement the Common Lectionary. Butcher provides four readings per week, but includes extra-biblical books such as the Gospels of Thomas, Peter, and Mary Magdalene, along with other early church documents such as the Didache and the Secret Book of James.[74]

One could cynically view lectionary-making as big business. On the other hand, it can be seen somewhat positively as a serious attempt to find new ways to tell our ancient story.

---

[72] You can learn more about the lectionary at www.seasonofcreation.com. This site tells the story of the season, as well as providing a vast array of resources for its use.

[73] Bandy's *Introducing the Uncommon Lectionary* is available from Abingdon Press.

[74] Butcher's book *An Uncommon Lectionary* is available from Polebridge Press.

Appendix 2 – Listing of Scriptures by Biblical Order

Genesis 1:1–2:4a (4b–25)	Advent 1
Genesis 9:8–17	Advent 3
Genesis 12:1–9	Epiphany 1
Genesis 15:1–6	Epiphany 2
Genesis 21:1–7	Christmas Day
Genesis 21:9–21	Epiphany 4
Genesis 32:22–31	Transformativa 16
Genesis 33:1–20	Transformativa 17
Genesis 37:1–11	Transformativa 3
Genesis 37:12–20, (21–24), 25–27, (28a), 28b–36	
	Transformativa 4
Genesis 38:11–26	Transformativa 2
Genesis 39:1–20 (40:6–23)	Transformativa 5
Genesis 41:17–40	Transformativa 6
Genesis 43:1–5, 15, 44:1–4, 14–18, 24–34,	
or 43:1 – 44:34	Transformativa 7
Genesis 45:1–15	Transformativa 8
Exodus 1:(1–5), 6–22	Transformativa 9
Exodus 2:1–10	Transformativa 10
Exodus 3:1–12a	Transformativa 11
Exodus 3:5–6, 13–15	Transformativa 1
Exodus 13:17–22 (14:10–31)	Transformativa 12
Exodus 16:1–15, 17:1–7	Transformativa 13
Exodus 20:1–17	Transformativa 14
Exodus 23:1–9	Transformativa 15
Exodus 26:30–37	Epiphany 3

Psalm 19	Epiphany 7
	Transformativa 19
Psalm 27	Epiphany 4
Psalm 30	Epiphany 5
Psalm 34	Transformativa 7
Psalm 46	Transformativa 2
Psalm 51	Lent 4
Psalm 57	Transformativa 4
Psalm 90	Lent 1
Psalm 99	Epiphany 1
Psalm 100	Epiphany 3
Psalm 102	Lent 2
Psalm 106	Easter Vigil
Psalm 121	Transformativa 10
Psalm 122	Transformativa 21
Psalm 124	Transformativa 9
Psalm 126	Last after Epiphany
Psalm 133	Transformativa 18
Psalm 137	Lent 5
Psalm 139:1–18	Epiphany 2
Psalm 148	Christmas Eve
Proverbs 1:20–33	Pentecost
Proverbs 8:1–11	Christmas Day
Proverbs 8:22–31	Advent 1
Ecclesiastes 3:1–8	Transformativa 3
Song of Songs (Solomon) 2:8–13	Epiphany 6
Isaiah 1:10–17	Transformativa 2
Isaiah 2:1–5	Advent 3
Isaiah 5:1–7	Transformativa 4

Isaiah 6:1–8	Transformativa 10
Isaiah 9:2–7	Christmas Eve
Isaiah 11:1–9	Epiphany 4
Isaiah 12:1–6	Transformativa 6
Isaiah 30:18–26	Epiphany 5
Isaiah 35:1–10	Epiphany 1
Isaiah 40:1–10	Advent 1
Isaiah 42:1–9	Epiphany 2
Isaiah 42:14–17	Transformativa 13
Isaiah 44:21–27	Transformativa 9
Isaiah 49:13–18	Christmas 1
Isaiah 52:13 – 53:12	Transformativa 8
Isaiah 58	Ash Wednesday
Isaiah 64:1–8	Transformativa 16
Isaiah 65:17–25	Easter
Isaiah 66:10–13	Transformativa 1
Jeremiah 1:4–10	Transformativa 5
Jeremiah 20:(1–6) 7–18	Transformativa 11
Jeremiah 31:31–34	Easter 2
Jeremiah 33:1–11	Last after Epiphany
Ezekiel 37:1–14	Epiphany 7
	Transformativa 19
Daniel 7:1–14	Transformativa 7
Hosea 11:1–11	Advent 2
Joel 2:1a, 12–16	Lent 1
Joel 2:25–29 (30–32)	Transformativa 18
Amos 2:10–12	Lent 3
Amos 5:10–15	Lent 4
Amos 7:10–15	Lent 2

Mark 3:(20–30), 31–35	Lent 3
Mark 4:35–41	Last after Epiphany
Mark 5:25–34	Epiphany 8
	Transformativa 22
Mark 7:14–23	Transformativa 24
Mark 7:24–30	Transformativa 18
Mark 10:46–52	Transformativa 9
Mark 12:13–17	Transformativa 13
Mark 14:12–50 (51–52)	Maundy Thursday
Mark 14:53 – 15:47	Good Friday
Luke 1:26–38	Transformativa 11
Luke 1:46–55	Advent 4
Luke 1:46–55	Transformativa 15
Luke 2:1–7 (8–20)	Christmas Eve
Luke 2:(1–7) 8–20	Christmas Day
Luke 2:29–38	Christmas 1
Luke 2:41–52	Christmas 1
Luke 3:1–14	Transformativa 14
Luke 3:15–18	Transformativa 23
Luke 4:10–13	Lent 2
Luke 4:16–21	Advent 3
Luke 5:1–11	Transformativa 10
Luke 6:20–26	Epiphany 7
	Transformativa 19
Luke 6:27–36	Transformativa 24
Luke 6:37–42	Transformativa 25
Luke 7:36–50	Ash Wednesday
Luke 8:49–56	Lent 5
Luke 10:25–37	Easter 5

Luke 12:22–32	Epiphany 5
Luke 13:10–17	Transformativa 12
Luke 15:1–10	Easter 2
Luke 15:11–32	Easter 3
Luke 18:9–14	Easter 4
Luke 19:1–10	Transformativa 17
Luke 19:28–40	Palm/Passion
Luke 21:5–19	Transformativa 26
Luke 22:14 – 23:56	Palm/Passion
Luke 23:26–31	Lent 4
Luke 24:1–11	Easter 1
Luke 24:13–35	Easter 4
John 1:1–5	Advent 1
John 1:(1–5), 6–18	Epiphany 1
John 1:43–50	Epiphany 2
John 2:1–12	Epiphany 7
	Transformativa 19
John 2:13–22	Transformativa 20
John 3:1–17	Transformativa 16
John 4:5–42	Epiphany 6
John 6:1–15	Epiphany 3
John 6:35–40	Epiphany 4
John 8:1–11	Transformativa 15
John 9:1–41	Transformativa 21
John 11:1–44	Easter Vigil
John 12:20–26	Easter Vigil
John 14:1–4	Easter Vigil
John 15:9–17	Transformativa 5
John 20:1–10	Easter

John 20:11–18	Easter 2
John 20:19–23	Easter 3
John 20:24–29	Easter 4
John 21:1–14 (15–19)	Easter 6
Acts 2:1–21	Pentecost
Acts 2:42–47	Transformativa 3
Acts 8:26–40	Transformativa 8
Acts 9:1–19	Easter 4
Acts 9:36–43	Transformativa 2
Acts 10:34–43	Transformativa 7
Acts 11:1–18	Easter 5
Acts 16:9–15	Transformativa 6
Acts 16:16–34	Transformativa 4
Romans 3:19–28	Ash Wednesday
Romans 5:(1–5) 6–11	Transformativa 23
Romans 7:15–25a	Epiphany 6
Romans 8:14–22 (23–25)	Advent 3
Romans 8:31–39	Transformativa 8
Romans 10:5–17	Transformativa 26
Romans 12:9–21	Transformativa 24
1 Corinthians 1:23–25	Easter 7
1 Corinthians 2:6–13	Epiphany
1 Corinthians 11:23–28	Transformativa 13
1 Corinthians 13	Christmas Day
2 Corinthians 4:6–10	Transformativa 6
2 Corinthians 5:16–21	Easter
Galatians 2:(15–18) 19–21	Transformativa 22
Galatians 3:23–28	Transformativa 15
Galatians 5:1–6	Easter 5

Appendix 3 – Calendar of Key Liturgical Dates 2010-2020

Year	Sundays after the Epiphany	Ash Wednesday	Easter
2010	6	February 17	April 4
2011	9	March 9	April 24
2012	7	February 22	April 8
2013	5	February 13	March 31
2014	8	March 5	April 20
2015	7	February 25	April 5
2016	5	February 10	March 27
2017	8	March 1	April 16
2018	6	February 14	April 1
2019	8	March 6	April 21
2020	7	February 26	April 12

Year	Pentecost	Sundays after Pentecost	Advent 1
2010	May 23	26	November 28
2011	June 12	23	November 27
2012	May 27	26	December 2
2013	May 19	27	December 1
2014	June 8	24	November 30
2015	May 24	26	November 29
2016	May 15	27	November 27
2017	June 4	25	December 3
2018	May 20	27	December 2
2019	June 9	24	December 1
2020	May 31	25	November 29

References

Biblical translations cited (other than those by individuals, which are listed below by author's name):

IB – *The Inclusive Bible* © 2007 by Priests for Equality.

NRSV – *New Revised Standard Version* © 1989 by the Division of Christian Education of the National Council of Churches of Christ in the USA.

TEV – *Good News Bible – Today's English Version*, Second Edition © 1992 American Bible Society.

TNIV – *Today's New International Version*, © 2001, 2005 International Bible Society.

Abbott, Margie RSM. *Sparks of the Cosmos: Rituals for Seasonal Use.* Unley, South Australia, Mediacom Education, 2001.

Aldredge-Clanton, Jann. *In Search of the Christ-Sophia: an Inclusive Christology for Liberating Christians.* Mystic, CT: Twenty-third Publications, 1995.

Blakeny, Raymond Bernard, trans. *Meister Eckhart: A Modern Translation.* New York: Harper and Brothers, 1941.

Bonneau, Normand. *The Sunday Lectionary: Ritual Word, Paschal Shape.* Collegeville, MN: Liturgical Press, 1998.

Borg, Marcus. *Reading the Bible Again for the First Time.* San Francisco: Harper, 2002.

Borg, Marcus. *The Heart of Christianity: Rediscovering a Life of Faith.* San Francisco: Harper Collins, 2004.

Cady, Susan, Marian Ronan, Hal Taussig. *Wisdom's Feast: Sophia in Study and Celebration.* San Francisco: Harper and Row, 1989.

Chilton, Bruce. *Rabbi Jesus: an Intimate Biography.* New York: Doubleday, 2000.

Cochran, Shelley. *The Pastor's Underground Guide to the Revised Common Lectionary: Year A.* St. Louis: Chalice Press, 1995.

Cohen, Leonard. *Stranger Music.* Toronto: McClelland and Stewart, 1993.

Countryman, L. William and M.R. Ritley. *Gifted by Otherness: Gay and Lesbian Christians in the Church.* Harrisburg, PA: Morehouse, 2001.

Crossan, John Dominic. *Jesus: a Revolutionary Biography.* San Francisco: Harper, 1994.

Douglas-Klotz, Neil. *Prayers of the Cosmos: Meditations on the Aramaic Words of Jesus.* San Francisco: Harper, 1990.

Fiorenza, Elisabeth Schüssler. *In Memory of Her: a Feminist Theological Reconstruction of Christian Origins.* New York: Crossroad, 1985.

Fox, Matthew. *A Spirituality Named Compassion.* Rochester, VT: Inner Traditions, 1999.

Fox, Matthew. *Creation Spirituality: Liberating Gifts for the Peoples of the Earth.* San Francisco: Harper, 1991.

Fox, Matthew. *Creativity: Where the Divine and the Human Meet.* New York: Jeremy P. Tarcher/Putnam, 2002.

Fox, Matthew. *Meditations with Meister Eckhart.* Santa Fe: Bear and Co., 1983.

Fox, Matthew. *Original Blessing: A Primer in Creation Spirituality* Santa Fe, New Mexico: Bear and Co., 1983.

Fox, Matthew. *Passion for Creation: the Earth–Honoring Spirituality of Meister Eckhart.* Rochester, VT: Inner Traditions, 2000.

Fox, Matthew. *The Coming of the Cosmic Christ.* San Francisco: Harper & Row, 1988.

Funk, Robert W., Roy W. Hoover, and the Jesus Seminar. *The Five Gospels: the Search for the Authentic Words of Jesus.* New York: MacMillan, 1993.

Habel, Norman, ed. *Readings from the Perspective of Earth: The Earth Bible 1.* Cleveland: Pilgrim Press, 2000.

Harvey, Andrew. *Son of Man: The Mystical Path to Christ.* New York: Jeremy P. Tarcher, 1999.

Heschel, Abraham. *The Prophets.* New York: Harper Collins, 2001.

His Holiness the XIV Dalai Lama. *The Four Noble Truths.* Translated by Geshe Thupten Jinpa. London: Thorsons, 1997.

Peterson, Eugene H. *The MESSAGE: The Bible in Contemporary Language.* Colorado Springs: NavPress, 2002.

Phillips, J.B. *The New Testament in Modern English.* London: Geoffrey Bles, 1960.

Schwarzentruber, Mike. *The Emerging Christian Way: Thoughts, Stories, and Wisdom for a Faith of Transformation,* (Kelowna, BC: Copper House, 2006.

Seasons of the Spirit: Congregational Life–Pentecost 2, 2005. Kelowna, BC: Wood Lake Books, 2005.

Williams, Michael E., ed. *The Storyteller's Companion to the Bible, Vol. Two – Exodus–Joshua.* Nashville: Abingdon, 1992.

Williams, Michael E., ed. *The Storyteller's Companion to the Bible, Vol. Four – Old Testament Women.* Nashville: Abingdon, 1993.

Wilson, Lois Miriam. *Miriam, Mary, and Me – Women in the Bible: Stories Retold for Children and Adults.* Kelowna, BC: Northstone, 1992.

About the author

Donald Schmidt was born and raised in British Columbia, Canada, where he attended worship and Sunday school in both the Anglican Church and United Church of Canada. He received two undergraduate degrees from Montreal's McGill University, a BA in comparative religion in 1981 and a Bachelor of Theology in 1984, following these with an MDiv from United Theological College (also in Montreal) in 1986 and a Doctor of Ministry from San Francisco's Wisdom University in 2006.

After moving to New York, Donald was ordained in the United Methodist Church in 1988 in New York, and has served churches in Quebec, New York, Vermont, and Hawai'i. He is currently a minister with the United Church of Christ in Washington state.

In addition to parish ministry, Rev. Schmidt has worked as a writer and editor of church resources for over fifteen years, writing both curriculum and worship resources for all ages, which have been used throughout the English-speaking world. He has also written a number of church songs that have been recorded by a variety of groups, and appeared in publications in Canada, the United States, and Australia.

He has taught church history, worship and preaching, and church dynamics at the Henry Opukaha'ia Center for Pacific Theological Studies. He continues to edit church resources, writes for several publications such as *Clergy Journal* and the *Minister's Annual Manual*, and is a consultant on a new biblical translation with the United Methodist Publishing House.

When he has spare time he likes to spend it knitting, walking, reading, making music, basket-weaving, or watching movies with his partner.

Please feel free to contact Donald with feedback about this book at kahudonald@clearwire.net. Also, check out www.emergingword.com.

www.ingramcontent.com/pod-product-compliance
Lightning Source LLC
Chambersburg PA
CBHW030005110426
42736CB00040BA/515